Journey of Hope

Jasmine Carol

Dillie Road Books

Dillie Road Books
8581 Santa Monica Blvd Suite 565
West Hollywood CA 90069
https://www.dillieroadbooks.com

Scripture quotations are from the King James Version, also known as the King James Bible, sometimes as the English version of 1611, or simply the Authorized Version.

First Dillie Road Books softcover edition September 2021

Journey
of
Hope

Table of Contents

Foreward

I was first attracted to the author of this book when I was fourteen years of age. Her beautiful long hair and appearance attracted me, but as I came to know her inner self, I encountered the most beautiful person. Our shared journey of hope began as sweethearts in high school, and we have navigated life together ever since. Jasmine is a wonderful mother, grandmother, and great grandmother—but best of all, she is my life partner and the love of my life.

A few years ago, Jasmine had this very deep and persistent feeling in her inner being that she needed to share life experiences from her childhood. Not to simply describe the hardships of growing up in a transient family and with persistent poverty, but to communicate there is hope—even when there doesn't appear to be any. When a person experiences eternal hope, not even the most dire of circumstances can extinguish it.

Trent

Prologue

Everyone has a story. Some are happier, some are easier, some are difficult. Others reveal remarkable success while others reveal great tragedy.

This is the story of my childhood. I grew up in an extremely poor transient family with eleven other siblings. Most of the time we were destitute, and our family relations were difficult—eventually damaging in many aspects. Many facets of my story have been difficult for me to write, and there are some childhood experiences I have chosen to not describe in detail.

Yet, it was a journey of hope. I am not sharing my story with you to portray an abject childhood, the effects of severe poverty, and the despair that comes with familial dysfunction. I am compelled to share my story to offer hope. I would not be here, on this earth, if not for the love and mercy of God. He has worked many miracles in my life and the lives of my family members. God offers His blessings and the gift of eternal life to everyone.

This morning the world is quiet, like a lovely photo, but larger. I am on our house porch, enclosed in windows, sharing the company of my sweet husband, Trent, of sixty years. The view is almost surreal. Snow thinly blankets the ground and the metal roofs of the buildings and barn on our simple farm. The trees stand silent, with only a few left-over, brown, curled, clinging leaves fluttering in the whisper of breeze.

Movement is almost imperceptible. Even the winter birds are still, not flicking or fluffing their feathers in the maze of tree limbs or darting from branch to branch. Trent looks at his phone and reads unpleasant political information. I tighten the sash on my long, thick, pink, soft, cuddly robe and go into the kitchen to grind some nicely roasted coffee beans for a fresh pot of coffee.

While the coffee is perking in its glass carafe, I remove the clean laundry from the dryer, and move the wet clothing from the washing machine to the dryer. After folding the lint-free clothing, I return to the kitchen to enjoy my cup of coffee.

I wish my mother had some of these conveniences when I was a child.

Blue Baby

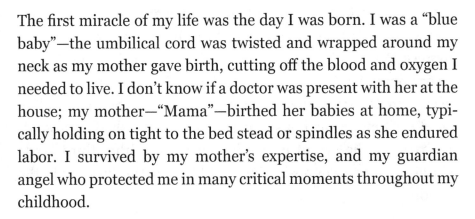

The first miracle of my life was the day I was born. I was a "blue baby"—the umbilical cord was twisted and wrapped around my neck as my mother gave birth, cutting off the blood and oxygen I needed to live. I don't know if a doctor was present with her at the house; my mother—"Mama"—birthed her babies at home, typically holding on tight to the bed stead or spindles as she endured labor. I survived by my mother's expertise, and my guardian angel who protected me in many critical moments throughout my childhood.

I thank God that He gave me life. With Mama's care and her rich milk, I thrived. I was the sixth child, having two older brothers and three older sisters. Eventually more babies would come yielding a family with twelve children—six girls and six boys.

I'm not sure what Daddy did when babies were born. He was meek and gentle and rarely spoke.

Daddy was twenty-one and Mama was fifteen years old when they were married in the middle of The Great Depression. They never talked about their childhoods. What I discovered about their early years was gleaned from random statements that popped up in conversations in my adult years.

Daddy's father, "John Henry" was of Native American heritage. The term used throughout my childhood to describe indigenous people was Indian (in addition to slurs I won't mention). I often have wondered how Daddy's mother met John Henry and married him in the days when the bigotry towards Native Americans was intense and the norm. Daddy's mother was not Native American. I don't know how many children Grandma and John Henry had, but Daddy was one of them.

The marriage of Grandma Miller and John Henry did not last. When Daddy was around eight years of age, his father left one evening and never returned. Why his father vanished is a mystery. Perhaps Daddy's father was killed or fled for his life; I'll never know. Daddy's mother, Grandma Miller, remarried before he was ten. His stepfather was not going to have a boy with Indian blood sleeping in his house, so Daddy was banished to sleep in the barn. At the age of twelve he left home with a third-grade education in tow, supposing he would have better luck out in the world.

Daddy never learned to read or write—a fact he always tried to keep secret—and could only sign his name with an "X." Many young men of those times lacked opportunity to learn to read or write. Daddy's deficiency in confidence masked his keen intelligence.

Mama's family was primarily of Irish descent. Her parents had saved a considerable amount of money with plans to build a house in Arkansas. Mama was barely a toddler at eighteen months of age when the second wave of the Spanish Flu—the global pandemic also called The Plague—struck the United States, killing her parents and newly born sister. Only Mama and her seven-year-old brother survived. Distant relatives arrived by horse and carriage, adopted Mama and her brother, and then returned to Oklahoma. Mama's mother by adoption was the person I came to know as Grandma Holland.

When Mama was three years old. Grandma Holland told her and her brother to put on their coats. She gave a satchel to Mama's brother and sent the two of them away from the house. Mama and her brother wandered about for some time, not knowing where to go. Eventually, Grandma Holland came and found them and told them they could come back home.

After the money from Mama's parents had been spent, the adopted parents returned to court, attempting to undo the adoption. The judge refused their request, stating "you spent the money; you take care of them." Shortly thereafter, Mama and her brother were sent to live with Grandma Holland's mother for a brief time.

Grandma Holland's mother and father were deaf and had been since her birth. When Grandma Holland was a child, her father had an altercation with a neighbor. Later, the neighbor came to their house, and her father—unable to hear—interpreted the man's intent as deadly. Her father shot and killed the neighbor. Soon after it became known to him that the law was coming for him, and he fled. Grandma Holland never saw him again.

Mama memory of her time at her grandmother's was pleasant, but eventually Mama and her brother returned to live with Grandma Holland.

Grandma Holland and her husband conceived five children after adopting Mama and her brother. Mama was five years old when her first stepbrother was born. Soon after the fifth child was born, Grandma Holland's husband allegedly committed suicide by jumping off a bridge. The hat he wore was found on the bridge railing with a suicide note underneath. Grandma Holland suspected that he didn't commit suicide but staged it so he could start a new life without the responsibility of several children.

Mama experienced another life-altering tragedy when she was six years of age. Her brother had taken on work at the nearby oil rigs, and one day his clothes got caught in some machinery. He died a brutal death at only twelve years old. Mama was thoroughly devastated.

By the time Mama was eleven years of age, she took on the role of "mother" to her step siblings while Grandma Holland worked other jobs to support the six children. At school one day, Mama's stepbrother was being bullied by a group of boys. He was pushed to the ground, and she flew into the fray! Her long golden hair flying wildly, she rushed the main bully, punching and kicking, and darting about so the boys could not grab her hair. The grandfather of one of the bullies saw the fight and came out shouting—cheering for my mother. "Get him, Thelma! Get him!"

And she did. Mama always protected her own.

Sadly, Mama was never made to feel like she was truly "one of the family" and frequently felt alone throughout her childhood. A tension developed between Mama and Grandma that increased over time—though later in life they developed an appreciation for each other. Mama was made to quit school early to address the family needs, but she never lacked in ability or knowledge. She developed magnitudes of courage and resilience that few people possess.

One night, when barely a teenager, she attended a nearby Pentecostal tent revival. The message of the gospel spoke to her, and she accepted the grace of God in that moment. The love and reality of God was deeply embedded in her soul; her faith would become a foundation for her teachings to us children.

Mama was short in stature, strikingly beautiful, exceptionally smart, and strong in character. Daddy was quite handsome with dark hair and olive skin and a muscular wiry build. When they met, the physical attraction and similar hardships they had experienced yielded a brief courtship before they decided to take on life together with the hope of a better future.

My sister Rachel was born a little over a year before me while my parents were on the road. They had traveled to California to see my Grandma Holland and as soon as my parents reached her house, the doctor was called. Rachel had decided it was time to come into the world. She was so beautiful, with dark hair and dark, sparkly eyes. I wish Rachel's life had been as beautiful as she was. Throughout life, she was always so vulnerable to aggressive and cruel people who took advantage of her soft heart.

When my parents returned from California, they moved into the old two-story house where I was born soon after.

It was the first of fourteen houses I lived in by the time I was eighteen years of age.

Old Tom

Not long after my birth we moved from the home where I was born to a lovely, large antediluvian country house that had two large rooms. I never knew why we moved; we just did and usually with little notice. This second home is where I became aware of the world.

I remember it because that was where my mind bloomed into the acknowledgement and reality of the tangible world. I was real, and so was the world. Every person has that moment when they become aware of themselves and the world around them. Some people don't remember that specific moment. I do. I was walking in the grass on a path toward the two-story house and saw my brother Kevin. He was involved in some interaction with some of the other kids and was too busy to notice me. My five older siblings thought I was too young to play games with them.

My oldest sister and brother, Breanne and Randall, were in early elementary school and walked a gravel road for two miles to attend classes. They were a little frightened when they had to cross the large body of water near the old schoolhouse. When it rained, Mama gave them a bag to carry so that when they came home from school, they could try to capture crawdads from the side ditches. Neither of them enjoyed this routine. Any crawdads captured would be our supper.

On another occasion, Randall got his shirt caught on an object that protruded from an upstairs window and almost hung himself.

Not far from our house was a large tent with dirt floors and rough chairs. This was "church" where people would sing and sit listening to old gospel preaching.

One day we were banished to the outdoors. A doctor wearing a black suit arrived with his leather bag. I tried to peek in the window, standing on my tip toes, hoping to see what was happening. But I couldn't see. Mama was having another baby.

Mama never made an issue about having babies, but eventually I figured out that must have been why the strange doctor was allowed in with Mama and Daddy. We never knew when a new baby was born; Mama was secretive about it with us kids. I wished to have been included in some part in the birth of my younger siblings—to have been shown the new baby, to touch his cheek, see her eyes, and be a part of the baby's entrance into the world. I wonder if we children would have been emotionally closer had we each of us been included in celebrating the arrival of a younger sibling.

This second house is where I came to know of our neighbor "Old Tom," as we children called him. After the war, there were men called "hobos." Many "rode the rails" without jobs, carrying long sticks or tree branches with handkerchiefs or other items tied to the end to carry whatever they had. They were homeless and penniless and looked for people who would give them food.

Mama didn't name him "Old Tom." We kids did, and not meaning any disrespect—we felt compassion for him even though he lived in an actual house. He suffered with alcoholism, and we would see or hear him at night sometimes when he returned, drunken, from town.

Frequently Old Tom came to our house and respectfully asked for something to eat. As poor as we were, often with only beans and home-made rolls for dinner, she never turned Tom away. As we children watched, wide-eyed and silent, Mama would politely instruct Tom to wait on the porch. Then she would prepare a plentiful plate of food, taking time to cover it nicely with paper or cloth. She would emerge from the house, and with a friendly, respectful smile, graciously hand the plate to Old Tom as if it were the most normal thing in the world. We witnessed the value of sharing, of respect, and learned that all people were of equal worth. No one was better than anyone else.

On one occasion, waiting politely on our porch for a plate of food, Old Tom took a small piece of wood and carved out a little horse for my brother, Kevin.

And then one night, as Old Tom was returning to his home from the bar after his usual indulgences, he was attacked. Some-one knifed him in the back, and Old Tom died. We were incredibly saddened when we heard the tragic news about his horrible, unbelievably cruel, and violent death. Sometimes, we children would look over at Old Tom's empty house and feel sad. I hope he had the fortune of experiencing the love of Jesus before he passed from this world. Drunk or not, Jesus wants to save everyone.

Growing Pains

Soon, we moved again, this time to a small, two-room, shanty house with a tiny porch. This third house had a large, round, open well in the backyard, surrounded by rocks. The rocks were large enough to sit on and helped to keep us from falling into the cavernous hole. The water from that well was used for drinking, washing dishes, laundry, bathing, and whatever else required water.

In the 1940s, polio was prevalent in society, eventually leading up to the worst outbreak in our nation's history in 1952. Some died from it, and various levels of paralysis were common. One day I could not get up from where I was sitting as I watched my siblings play baseball. My legs would not support me, and I could not walk. Stuck, I sat there long after my siblings had finished their game and returned to the house. Finally, thinking something was wrong, Mama sent my sister down and she carried me to the house. I couldn't walk for several days. I was thankful beyond measure when I could walk again. Mama said that I just had "growing pains." Whether it was polio or growing pains, I know it was another moment where an angel of God was watching over me.

There were many questions during that time as to what caused polio. Some people ended up wearing braces on their legs so they could walk. It has been suggested that there was a link between the polio outbreak and a chemical that was being used in agriculture. No one seemed to know what caused the dreaded situation.

Years later I learned that missionaries in South America were able to help people with polio by placing them on teeter-totters, moving them up and down on their backs, to keep their lungs from getting clogged. This simple procedure saved their lives!

None of us liked living in the old shanty house. Before long, we moved to another old house a short distance away—the fourth house I lived in.

The North Walnut House

The fourth house I lived in was an old white house located at the end of the dirt road on North Walnut—the "North Walnut" house. I always wondered about the people that had built the old houses we lived in, so many decades before us—their families, their dreams, what tough times did they encounter, and what eventually happened to them.

The North Walnut house was our home for a much longer time than became typical for us. Daddy worked at the railroad, and Mama was home caring for all her children. The house was larger and better, having two bedrooms, a kitchen with a cast iron stove, and a living room. We even had a buffet that held dishes. It lacked running water, as most of our homes did, but we didn't know any different. There was also a spacious front porch that we enjoyed. There were many good experiences in this house, and some not so good, but we children had much fun and were sweetly innocent. I loved living in the house on North Walnut; it was the best place I ever lived as a child.

The house also had a wooden ice box that held large blocks of ice whenever we had enough money to buy ice. When you wanted to buy ice, you placed an ice card in your window and the man who drove around selling ice, brought you a large ice chunk in a cube. He carried it with a metal contraption called ice tongs that were adjustable to accommodate the size of the ice that was ordered. It was not an easy job, carrying those heavy, dripping, chunks of ice, and the man usually carried it hunched over a little, and his legs were a bit bowed.

It was a privilege when we were able to pay about a quarter for the large chunk of ice. It meant that we could enjoy having some iced tea to drink, and that was a real treat! Mama would make a large, galvanized tin pail of iced tea, sweetened with a little sugar, then place it on a low bench on our front porch so we children could help ourselves to it. We so enjoyed the refreshing treat of tea!

On the wood slats boards of that same porch, I can still picture my younger, golden-haired brother—still a toddler—intently studying a worm, curious about the worm's ability to continue living as two creatures when pulled apart. How would my sweet, innocent little brother become involved in such terrible incidents later in life? Mama said he was mentally deficient and was always trying to find help for him. He was so vulnerable; later in life he was led astray by a very conniving woman. She was so beautiful that no one could believe she was so malevolent.

We children helped Mama and did our chores, but we spent most of our time playing. We created countless activities and were always occupied with discovery and play. We chased fireflies and squashed them to make incandescent jewelry that glowed on our fingers and clothes in the dark of the night. That was our wealth—golden, flashing, and free. We spent our days jumping rope, playing hopscotch for hours, racing each other, climbing trees, picking berries and nuts, coloring in color books, playing cowboys and Indians, fishing, and swimming. In the yard was a large tree, a distance from the peach tree and away from the creek. I loved climbing this tree and hanging upside down from its limbs. All of us children created amazing fun that developed our minds and expanded our imaginations.

We were allowed to just be children—and that was an indescribable blessing. One embarrassing memory is a moment in which I climbed into the spindled baby bed in the living room and enjoyed drinking the milk from one of the younger baby's bottles.

Mama encouraged "outside" activities—weather permitting. With rain or storms, we played indoors, and our options were distinctly different.

We girls sat on the floor and designed small houses for our small dolls to live in. We divided the rooms with cardboard partitions or whatever we could find to create some semblance of a house, and played with little dolls of rubber, plastic, or paper dolls. Most of our paper dolls were carefully cut from old, thrown-out catalogs that had been salvaged from nearby trash cans or retrieved from the local dump we would explore on occasion. On some occasions, new catalogs were found, and we excitedly searched the pages for our new paper dolls. We also enjoyed building houses for our paper dolls.

My brothers created their own diverse universe of crashing and racing cars and trucks and sewn-up strange-looking sock men who spent time beating each other up—the sock men, that is. Aside from an occasional observation, I wasn't interested in their world view of toys. I loved baby dolls. One of my dreams was to have a tiny rubber baby doll. It was about one or two inches high, with little pink legs and arms. I so desperately wanted that little baby doll—but I never got one. Many years later in life, I was blessed with granddaughters. When they were small, I tried to interest them in the multitudes of baby dolls in the stores. But as time moves on, so does the interests of children and society. Baby dolls once had their day, but the interests of young children today are elsewhere.

We children enjoyed firecrackers! One year, I followed my siblings to the small fire-cracker tent. It was the first time I was allowed to tag along, and I felt quite privileged to be able to participate. Inside the tent I excitedly looked over all the colorful firecrackers and rockets and sparklers. With one lone penny in my hand, I pointed to some firecrackers and bravely asked the seller "How much are your penny firecrackers?" I was privy to the laughter and joking of my siblings all the way home for thinking I could purchase some fireworks for a penny.

On hot and humid summer nights, we children would sometimes carry our blankets outside to the yard to sleep under the star-filled sky, where it was cooler than in the old house. We weren't concerned about mosquitos and ticks and other little pests. One night I pantomimed a story I created, trying to portray a wonderland of the beauty and hope in God's world. I put my heart and soul into this venture, wanting to encourage my younger siblings, considering the constant challenges our family faced. Later in life, my younger brother Stephen told me that his memory of this moment lifted his spirits immensely when he was in the military, stationed in Germany.

Once, on my walk home from school during my first-grade year, I saw my oldest brother, Randall, as he was working his paper-route job. He noticed me, paused, then came over to me. He took me into the ice-cream store I had just walked by and bought me an ice-cream cone for a nickel. That was a fortune in those days when we were so poor. One night, I even awoke from sleep, sitting straight up and licking a huge ice cream cone. I continued to lick and lick, then slowly became aware that I was clasping nothing, licking only an imaginary, invisible cone.

Randall worked so hard each day, throwing newspapers into the yards of those who could afford such conveniences. He was always very committed to his jobs. Eventually he saved enough to buy a bike, which was a tremendous help for delivering newspapers. Unfortunately, he had a terrible accident on the bike, and there was great concern he would lose his arm. By God's grace the doctors were able to save his arm.

On one occasion I managed to embed a fishhook in my foot. A neighbor came down and cut the hook's wire, then pulled it out backwards from my skin. Mama rubbed iodine or hydrogen peroxide on the wound, as those were medications, she used a lot for our injuries. Mama knew of many methods to help us heal. She placed cooked onions on our chests when we had a cold or congestion. She gave us each a spoonful of sugar with some turpentine for worms. She would tape a cloth filled with vinegar over a wart to remove it. If we had a stye in our eye, she would place a moist tea bag on the eyelid and the stye would vanish within a day or two. Mama taught me to heal the large, round, red and itchy ringworm on my knee by rubbing the green substance from the inner walnut shell on it; my knee was healed in about three days. Fortunately, it was the time of year when the walnut shells were just falling off the trees and the husks were bumpy green and fresh.

It was while living at this house that I contracted the three-week measles, or "hard measles," that result from the Rubeola virus. People feared this dangerous form of measles; at the least it often scarred and pitted the skin. More severe outcomes included blindness, hearing loss or deafness, brain damage, and death due to respiratory and neurologic complications.

Mama had me stay in bed while I had a fever. She covered my face with a red cloth to protect my skin from pitting or scarring that could occur from the severe and unbearable itching caused by the disease. When I could eventually get out of bed and wander about the house, she didn't allow me to go near the windows to protect my eyes from sunlight. Mama wanted us children to be strong, and she did all she could to protect our health and make us strong.

Let It Snow

One of the most fun things we children did while living in the North Walnut house was making snowmen. After an ample snowfall, we bundled up in our second-hand winter coats and excitedly headed outside. It was always better when the structure of the snow was fluffy and soft; the snowballs we rolled were used to build tri-ball snow people. Each one of us began by making a small, tightly packed snowball, laid it on a promising area of snow, then rolled it until it reached the size desired for the snowman.

Calculations were important to create a snow person that was sturdy and would stand stoically and impressively for as long as possible. Each ball of snow was rolled separately, packed tightly, until it was proportional in size to the other balls used for the body and head. The bottom one had to be structured strong and large enough to hold the middle ball and then the top ball. Rolling and lifting these large balls of snow was difficult and sometimes required help from another kind sibling. If chunks of snow fell off while stacking the large balls of snow, new snow had to be carefully patted into the hole to keep your snow person from collapsing into nothing but a mound of snow.

While building snowmen, the freezing temperatures would require us to take a pause to thaw our fingers and toes. We would run onto the porch for a little while, pull off our mittens, shake the snow from them, and warm ourselves up by the wood- burning iron stove. Then each of us would rush back out to work on our respective snow person. It was a challenging activity, but the intent to create meant you usually didn't recognize that your cheeks were red, that your lips were white and chapped, and that the air you were breathing was freezing on your nose and face. When the top ball, the head, was finally placed upon the other two balls—the bottom and the middle—it was time to place eyes, a nose, and mouth. Almost time to celebrate!

Next came the sticks for the side arms and the scarf around the neck and voila! Your very own snow person! Then you could indulge in whatever cleverness you wanted to add. My sisters' and my snow people were usually cute and cheerful, while my brothers' created snowmen that were fierce and frightening. Building snow people was not a job for the faint-hearted! It took a lot of work, and the bigger your sculpture of snow, the harder the job! However, the feeling of artistic accomplishment was huge!

Hours and hours were spent sledding, building impressively strong and large igloos, just working hard, being freezing cold, having loads of fun, and work. It was so exciting to sled down a long hill, turning the wooden handles skillfully, so you wouldn't crash into a creek or a tree, but then you had to grip the rope attached to the front of the sled and drag or pull it back up the long, long, hill.

As far as igloos were concerned, the work and design were not a small challenge. Assuming you wanted it to not collapse after you made it. Cutting the blocks from the snow, placing them in the correct position and place so they would hold the weight of the arched roof so the whole thing wouldn't cave in on you. And we accomplished it!

Mama even made party ice-cream out of the deep, clean snow! She would place the snow in a large, round, galvanized tub and then add canned milk and sugar. We had a party, even inviting neighbors to enjoy it with us. Mama was amazing!

In addition to throwing snowballs, building snowmen, constructing igloos, and hosting ice-cream parties, we did a lot of sledding.

We liked those old wooden sleds. The length of wood at the top of the sled could be shifted while in motion, enabling the rider to guide the sled along the desired trajectory. It was an exciting and fun challenge! One of our favorite hills presented an additional challenge; there was a deep creek at the bottom of the hill that required the sledder to exert significant effort to turn and slow the sled after the thrilling descent lest the journey careen into pain and misery. When the sled came to a stop, we dragged our sleds back to the top of the hill, huffing and puffing and ignoring our frozen fingers, resolved to experience again the short delight of speeding down the hill. Oh, what fun! The best sledding was when the path was smooth ice. Once my three sisters and I climbed aboard a single sled at the top of a slippery, packed snow-covered hill. The four of us were too many for the sled, and I slid off the back of the sled as it disembarked, leaving me sitting on the crest of the hill.

How I miss my sisters who have gone to be with Jesus and appreciate the ones who are still upon this earth. Love your family and others; share with all the truth of God's gift of eternal life so that when life on this earth is finished, you can be together again in heaven.

Duties and Deals

Of course, we had chores to do. Without them, how could we learn responsibility? As children, we did not see the advantages of such theology; each of us dreaded our turn. For many of the chores we paired with another sibling. One such chore was doing dishes. One of us would place the dishes in a pan of soapy water, then scrub each dish to remove the residue from the meal, then put the clean dish into a pan filled with clear water to rinse off the soapy suds. The other sibling would dry that dish with a dish towel. None of us enjoyed this chore. The next time it was a pair's turn to do the dishes, the two siblings exchanged positions and tasks. The washer became the dryer—and so forth.

Then, there was the boring and challenging chore of carrying water from the well in the backyard of the shanty house where we had previously lived to our current house. And now, the trek was farther.

Carrying buckets brimming with water was not delightful pageantry. Foremost, you did not want to fall into the large, round well that had no cover. After retrieving the coarse rope and attaching it to the bucket, you had to lower the bucket to the surface of the water, then coerce the rope in such a way that the bucket would tilt and begin to fill with water. Once filled, you had to exercise care to not twist up the rope and bucket, losing the water. Next was the challenge of pulling the heavy, filled bucket to the top of the well without dropping it. The large rocks surrounding the well assisted us, providing leverage for our thighs as we tightened them to pull on the rope and hoist up the bucket of water.

Then, the bucket, with the additional water weight, had to be carried in such a way that the water didn't all splash out before you reached the house. No one wanted to be drenched before they got the bucket to the low bench—or required to make the trip once more due to lost water.

Once you arrived at the house, you maneuvered the screen door with a foot or knee or elbow while maintaining the buckets' equilibrium, then proceeded into the house with the water haul. Mama was very considerate; she placed a low bench where the water buckets could be placed and easily used by the younger children. For drinking water, there was a dipper with a curved tin handle that rested on the rim of the bucket—all of us children drank from that dipper.

22

We children became very clever about exchanging the current chore assignments with other siblings, and that wasn't easy. You had to convince an interested party that it would, for some reason, be beneficial for them to trade "times" with you. Sometimes you might get an agreeable sibling to swap chores just because your appeal connected to their generosity. More frequently, if your explanation failed, you would have to up your offer or make some irresistible trade. A distant extravagant promise might work, but usually just once. In our family, your word best be honorable, or persecution might be in order. A distant promise was not forgotten. With several children in the mix, exchanging chores was even more challenging with competing offers. Amazingly, Mama kept track of each child's turn at the chores. And she always enforced the "clean-up after yourself" policy.

Godliness and Gratitude

Mama became an expert at anything she set her mind to and was exceptionally motivated. The demands of caring for a growing family while having few resources deter was a never-ending challenge—and she met it head-on. She refused to let scarcity define our dignity.

For the perpetual dirty laundry produce by active children, she set up a large, galvanized-metal tub full of soapy water—water that was retrieved from a well, transported by buckets, and then heated on a wood stove. She pushed and pulled and squeezed and wrung dirty clothes, towels, blankets, and quilts—sometimes needing to replace the now-dirty water with new soapy water. Some garments she scrubbed on an old wash board, rubbing them over the curvy, metal attachment. Then the metal tub would be emptied and filled with clean water to rinse the soap

from the laundry—another round of pushing and pulling and squeezing and wringing. Finally, the laundry was hung outside on clotheslines and sometimes spread over the bushes—no matter the season of year. In the summer, it would dry quickly and in the winter it would freeze stiff.

Mama ironed and ironed in those days. Given that we had no electricity, the iron was a heavy block of iron with a wooden handle. Heating it required placing it on the wood stove for several minutes—which required the wood stove to be full of wood and burning hot. She ironed clothes and bedding, taking time to reheat the iron as it cooled. on the wood stove until it was hot, then when it cooled, she set it on the stove to heat it again. Clothes were nicely folded. Beds were neatly made, or the bedding was folded and placed aside to retrieve at night when sleeping on the floor was required.

When lice were prevalent at school, Mama washed our hair in a bucket of kerosene. If someone mentioned a bed bug, Mama wiped down each side of every mattress with coal oil. I don't recall ever seeing a bed bug. Talcum powder was used prevalently—another tactic Mama used to repel bugs.

We children played well together, but when our tussles happened, verbal or physical, Mama corrected us. Her warnings were typically all it took to behave. She responded quickly and fairly, administering either judgement or, if the behavior were too dramatic, she could handily use a switch. Occasionally, if necessary, she brought out the big guns—a belt. We children did not arrogantly sass her.

People can argue about "switchings," and such, but I think Mama's methods of repercussions endowed us with a sense of considering our behavior before enacting it.

Mama kept things on the straight and narrow. She kept order and us kids benefitted by her fair justice, mercy, and faith in God. She taught us children how to live by the ten commandments along with the eleventh which was to encourage us children to obey the first ten. I am thankful that Mama taught us to honor what we say. To love and care about others without expecting anything in return. To be honest, never to steal, never to lie, work hard, and most of all, to follow God.

Daddy and Mama tried so amazingly to raise us kids well, teach us honor and decency, and God's truths.

By the grace of God, she took us all to church each Sunday, making sure we were all spiffed up out of respect for God's house. Then, with one or two babies in the baby buggy and the remaining children by her side, we walked for miles as she pushed the baby buggy—no matter the distance or the circumstances.

Mama also taught us to pray every night before we went to bed. There was a special prayer that she taught us, that I sometimes pray even to this day at bedtime.

Now I lay me down to sleep.
I pray, thee Lord, my soul to keep.
If I should die, before I wake,
I pray, thee Lord, my soul to take.

Regardless of the frequent conflict between Daddy and Mama, this North Walnut home saw more babies arrive, until there were ten of us children. I'm thankful Mama believed in God's Word and did not follow the outspoken Margaret Sanger. Sanger, in those days, was a popular voice. She promoted the thought that people should abort their babies. She also advocated a genetics-based approach to "breeding," stating abortion should be used for "the release and cultivation of the better racial elements in our society, and the gradual suppression, elimination and eventual extirpation of defective stocks—those human weeds which threaten the blooming of the finest flowers of American civilization." Was abortion as "birth control" the true goal of Sanger's worldview? Her words reveal something much more sinister.

Mama and Daddy couldn't comfortably afford so many children but thank God they didn't follow Sanger's worldview and begin exterminating their babies because of our poverty.

I am sure Sanger would have considered us "weeds" while she promoted the ideology that wealth equates to success and that aborting babies would bring about greater wealth and increase the possessions one could have.

Mama's life had never been easy. But she had faith in God, and she valued the lives of her babies—much more than financial wealth and possessions.

Over the years, some people had the audacity to ask Mama if she would give them some of her children, assuming she might be able to spare a couple since she had so many. Perhaps they weren't able to have children; whatever the reason, it was still sad that Mama was asked to give away some of her children.

Each one of my sisters were beautiful and my brothers, strong. We were all smart and capable. Mama and Daddy were so blessed to have such wonderful babies.

Living with Mama and Daddy in the North Walnut house, we children didn't know we were poor. We were 'poor' on the exterior, and couldn't afford the items that others had, but we were rich in the most important principles.

Not long ago, I read about a past president whose daughter was very privileged—she was about my age while I lived in the North Walnut house. For Christmas one year, her father bought her a baby grand piano, but this was not the gift that she wanted. She had her heart set on a train set and was so angry at the unwanted gift that she refused the piano and hastened to her room in disgust.

This was about the same time that I lingered after the last class was finished in grade school. After school was dismissed, a piano instructor came to teach piano to students whose parents could afford to pay for lessons. From a distance, I dreamed of such an opportunity as I observed the piano teacher attempting to instruct one of my classmates on how to play the piano. My classmate was bored, disinterested, and unappreciative. She sat on the piano bench unconcerned with the lessons. I stood there, my heart beating exuberantly, blood flowing through my whole body, my fingers aching to touch and play those beautiful, entrancing keys that made such beautiful sounds. I was tingling with desire to run my fingers over those keys, and it was difficult to hold myself back to just watch the scene. I couldn't afford such luxury and privilege, yet still I hungered to be the student sitting on the piano stool. I would slowly button up my coat, gather my school supplies, and camouflage my disappointment and a heavy cloud of tears as I walked home.

I never lost the desire I had that day in grade school to sit down at that piano and have the teacher instruct me to play those melodious keys.

The old house on North Walnut, at the end of the dirt road, by the creek, with the trees that we children climbed and the bats that stayed in the basement until night, when they flew out in a large group, where so much of my youth was spent, where God sprinkled miracles and angels in my life—these years were the best life I had as a child, even with the world in the shadow of war and having the ghost of peace. World War II had ended, and America was experiencing greater opportunity than before. Many Americans were growing wealthier. Not so much for my family. Daddy could not read or write and that did not benefit his job at the railroad. However, God did provide us with blessings.

Twelve Children

Suds were few in that old tub
Times were hard, so Mama scrubbed
Dresses, undies, socks and shirts
Vapored victory over dirt...

Beating at stiff, gray, coarse jeans—
No time—the mind—for idle dreams.
Battle fought—and only won—
Until we pulled a garment on!
    For what do children care of soil—
    Or understand poor Mama's toil?

We ran and jumped and slid and climbed
Dirt and rips ne'er entered mind
For life was sunshine, field, and trees
Playing "house" with dolls and teas.

Riding sticks fast as the wind!
Fighting pirates—and such men.
Creeping through the brush unseen
Knees and tummy stained with green.

Climbing up Jack's giant bean
Being knighted by the King!
Baking 'neath the sunny skies—
Muddy, molded, "pretend-pies"...
    Digging deep for treasure hidden—
    'Til darkness fell and we were bidden...

"Time to come in!" Mama called—
And in we trooped, both large and small.
Knowing if we lingered long,
The switch might twitch us for our wrong.

I would not from my mind erase
The beauty of my Mama's face—
As there she stood, screen door held
Wide until twelve children were inside.
    Twelve healthy, vibrant children there,
    Held in check by Mama's care.

The silver spoon had passed us by
But we laid claim to God's blue sky
Which canopied our childish schemes
And flung out star-inspiring dreams.

And smiled upon a creek to wade,
And stick-pole fishin' in the shade.
Though possessions were but few—
Wealthy—we—as up we grew!

Days of yonder, fraught with fun!
Apple-cheeked, beneath the sun—
Little children, did not see
How Mama's labors made us free.

Feeding the Multitudes

Since food was a luxury for us, we lived on a healthy diet of beans, beans and bread, beans and potatoes, beans, and beans. Mama always made certain we children had food—beans were our specialty, for which we thanked God. Mama always had a pot of beans boiling away on the stove, steam wafting through the house with a scent that we appreciated.

Mama could make the best buns in the world. She was a master bread maker. I loved watching her hands mixing, mashing, sculpting that ivory dough, and then beating it, pulling it, and pinching off pieces of dough that she could measure by touch or by eyeing it with her expert calculations. Then, she would dust the table with flour, dust the rolling pin and then rolling it with thin, fine flour, she would shape each ball and fit them, oiled, snugly together. After covering each tin to warmly rise the dough, she would then bake the round buns in the prepared pans and the old, warmed oven.

She just knew how to do it. And when those tall, fluffy, crispy-browned rolls were removed from the oven—well, what can I say? There just wasn't anything like them.

One night Daddy drove some of us to town, and we crept down the alley between the ice-cream store and the grocery store. Daddy left the car, and we could see him in the shadows looking through the garbage bin. Soon he returned with some food. I was thrilled to see a box of gold and red candy bars! With permission, I tore off a wrapper and bit into the delicate, delicious chocolate, savoring the sweet, silky taste. I had eaten some of it, savoring the flavor and texture, when I noticed some movement on the surface of the bar.

The chocolate bar had worms on it, and they too were covered with the brown, sweet chocolate. I showed the bar to Mama and Daddy, and they agreed that I should wipe off the worms. I was ecstatic that I didn't have to throw away the candy, so I knocked off the little thieves and ate the candy bar. So chocolatey delicious!

WORMS EATING MY DELICIOUS CHOCOLATE CANDY! BARS!

Another time, again in the dark of night, Daddy drove us a distance in the night, and we turned into a strange and frightening place which we were unfamiliar with. We stared at the grass in a field as the car lights shined in its circular pattern. Finally, thankfully, we came to a barn and a plump man came out of the darkness. Daddy got out of the car, and they disappeared for a while. We children were nervous waiting for not knowing what. The two men returned with bags full of old bread, rolls, and pies— food that the man had been going to feed to his pigs.

When we saw the bounty, we children were thrilled. The food was a blessing that we enjoyed for a while. God bless that generous man.

Cold Biscuit

Finally, I was allowed to go to school! I was so excited to attend school, just like my brothers and sisters did. However, going to school also revealed another dichotomy. Our clothes were often charity clothes; our very used shoes were brought to the house in boxes. Each pair went to whichever child they best fit, which is not to say they "fit." We often placed cardboard in the bottom of our shoes which already had worn soles. "School lunches" did not exist and each student was to bring their own lunch.

At home, Mama's bread, whether rolls or biscuits, were wonderful! She could make delicious biscuits, soft and fluffy and perfectly baked. With beans or without beans, they were fabulous. For school lunches, Mama provided each of us children with a freshly made biscuit, neatly wrapped in newspaper held in place by a piece of carefully tied twine, and with our name written on the newspaper.

On my first day at school, I walked into the classroom with my fellow students, and our teacher instructed us to place our lunches on a shelf in the small coat closet. I didn't notice the other lunch containers as I placed mine on the shelf. When it was lunchtime, the teacher retrieved the lunches from the closet and placed them on her desk. As she called out the name on each container, a student walked to the front of the class to claim their lunch. Suddenly my world changed.

I didn't see any little newspaper-tied bundles such as mine; I saw things I had never seen before. The students collected colorful tins with handles on them, and some of them opened one way, and some opened another. Some were shaped in squares of red and white and some were shaped with rounded tops with an assortment of color, some were metallic colors, most had little clips to open and close them. Then I heard my name called. I was so terribly embarrassed as I carried my simple, small package back to my desk in full view of all the other students.

While trying to be discrete, I watched in amazement as my classmates opened their containers, filled with all kinds of food and drink. They had real slices of store-bought bread with peanut butter and jelly, sandwiches thick with meats, and fresh fruits like apples. Milk to drink coupled with cookies. Some even had chocolate! Others had delicate cakes with white filling, wrapped in shiny, translucent paper. The bounty that emerged from the colorful tins surrounded me on the other students' desks was unbelievable.

Seeing the abundance and assortments of delicacies, I felt ashamed of my little, lowly, package with its coarse twine and newspaper that crumpled as I opened it to reveal my home-made, Mama-made-with-love, pale, brownish-white, biscuit. And the shame doubled, knowing the work Mama had done so I could take a lunch to school like the other students. Embarrassed, I tried to maintain a semblance of nonchalance as I nibbled my biscuit, hoping to make it last longer, my face down in shame.

The lunch protocol continued, each day more difficult, when the teacher called my name and I walked up to her desk at to retrieve my lonely newspaper-wrapped biscuit that paled in comparison with the impressive lunch pails and tins. I never lost the shame of carrying my little bundle back to my seat with all those curious eyes observing. But I didn't have the heart to explain how I felt to Mama. I knew it would hurt her and I wouldn't do that.

One day, as my classmates were busy picking and choosing through their generous lunches, the teacher quietly placed some items on my desktop and then moved imperceptibly, ghost-like, to several other desks, making a quick surreptitious gesture at each desk.

I was bewildered! A large chunk of bright, yellow, cheese and dried but black pieces of plump raisins that now sat on my desk. Obviously, she had placed them there. But why?

The perceptive teacher was a truly kind person. She observed that those of us children who had received this unexpected and unbelievable gift were unsure as to what we were to do with the food. She understood we would not benefit by calling attention to her wonderful deed. She keenly and pragmatically chose words to assure us to enjoy the lunch, as if we were no different from the other students. She saved us from shame.

The food was strange to eat, but delicious! Cheese and raisins were not on my family's scanty and undependable list of food items.

Shockingly, some of the most privileged students with their lavish lunches were irate and dissatisfied that some of us received a gift that they did not receive. I couldn't believe their response. They always had such an ample supply of food.

The extra food came each day and was a considerable blessing. There was some explanation about a program being initiated by the president to help the "under-privileged"—the significant count of displaced and needy Americans. I had no awareness of politics when I was in the first grade, but I thought this president man must be a kind and wonderful person.

Over the years, I've heard many debates about helping the poor. Even today I head "let them pull themselves up by their bootstraps." But I thank God for the food he supplied us. You weren't considered under-privileged in those days; you were considered shiftless if you didn't have a job, not matter how dedicated you were to looking for work.

The women who had gone to work during the war, found the extra money was helpful, and decided to keep their careers. Things changed drastically in many ways, and I honestly don't know that it helped the children and their families. The children spent a lot of time alone, and it has been my experience that in a family it helps to have a caretaker who isn't too tired or mentally exhausted from the demands required to have a successful job, to take care of the family.

I know that for myself, when I have been tired and focused, it has been difficult to listen and engage, much less embrace, the needs of my family. I wish others well. Many children, it appears, have done well when they were part of a working family. I've not researched the science. Maybe their parent's financial accomplishments created an easier and more successful educational career.

I do know my family would have better careers with funding available, but I don't know how that compares to a mother's attention, which is of immense value. I think it is necessary for parents to study the Scriptures to find answers for themselves. Corporate leaders would do well for others, if they were generous toward acknowledging the needs of families and included the family as a whole unit with consideration of finances and expectations, as well as the time involved in labor.

When Mama allowed me to spend time with some of my friends after school for a half-hour or so, I found most of the girls came from nice, clean, and in some cases, some of the more well-to-do neighborhoods. They even had snacks at home, but their houses were empty of life, and soon I wanted to just go back to my home—no snacks and no television, but Mama was there, brothers and sisters were there, and lots of life!

The availability of more opportune jobs was making people's lives such that they seemed to not want children, or only one or two children. Many of the children I knew at school lived in comfortable homes, but frequently it seemed to me their lives were sterile. Though I had no impressive possessions, I felt sorry for them.

Cold Biscuit

Cold biscuit made of flour and water and pain and love and care—
each morning wrapped in newspaper and tied with mama's flair.

How nice you looked in mama's hands—how soft and white and good,
how neat my bundle as I skipped so merrily to school.

Yet, the further, I, from home and closer to school grew,
the warmness of my mother's care began to fade from view.

In cuddly frocks and golden curls, from houses trim and neat,
boys and girls began to merge upon the busy street.

And in their hands were luncheon pails, whose colors seemed to glow,
and heavier and heavier my bundle seemed to grow.

Cold biscuit wrapped in newspaper, why do you try to hide?
When mama strove her love to give when wrapping you inside?

What traitor I, small and weak to now despise you so—
where is the sense of joy I had when mama tied your bow?

Why do I fault you now, at school, where went my heart so merry?
Why do I covet earnestly, a little pail to carry?

Little biscuit wrapped in love, so pleasant at the start!
How can you every morning tear my little heart apart?

Why every morning do you change into an enemy?
And every day when noon arrives, you twist the heart in me?

But never did that bundle change, to bring to me a smile,
and every lunch that journey seemed a trillion, lonely miles.

And every day I ate my bread as if I did not see
those gooey cakes and shiny fruits that quite surrounded me.

And sitting there, amongst those kids, I nibbled every bite—
allowing not myself to want their goodies soft and light.

Cold biscuit, wrapped in newspaper, for all the world to see—
how dry to swallow, when at lunch the kids all stare at me.

And yet, they do not comprehend, just cock a curious head—
as if they think it very strange I choose to eat just bread.

Pandora's box of sandwiches, with meat, or peanut butter—
The smells escaping heartily to make my taste-buds flutter.

One day, my teacher came around, and gave with ample measure—
raisins, cheese from government—to some of us a treasure!

Raisins! I stared at them puzzled, were they truly free?
Why would the government give out this prized commodity?

Cheese! I chewed each morsel carefully, my taste buds were enthralled!
I savored each exquisite bite, there were no crumbs at all!

The kids who ate from lovely pails, cast glances at my prize,
I found it hard to understand the message in their eyes.

Contempt? Oh, no, but envy. Perplexing me that day,
for every lunch so many had so much to throw away!

Their pails, with hinges and a lid, puddings, gleaming brown,
their sandwiches, their milk so white—to wash all their food down!

Cold biscuit, wrapped in newspaper, so bitter and so sweet,
how gave you me the sustenance to never say defeat?

Dreadful Assumptions

Mama instilled in us a strong work ethic and the ability to use our intellect. Life was great for us children, even with our poverty, but as we ventured out into society and school, we discovered a different dynamic. We children struggled in a society that frequently excluded poor people and heaped emotional abuse upon innocent victims of poverty. We experienced the snobbery that came with school—often from the teachers. The first grade wasn't too bad—the children were still innocent, and the first-grade teacher was so kind. However, some teachers were not nice at all and even went out of their way to hurt us. Throughout our school years, me and my siblings experienced multiple occasions of cruelty due to dreadful and lazy assumptions of some "educators" regarding our impoverished situation.

I remember my brother, Kevin, winning a photography contest. He was so excited and proud. Then the teacher took his award away and gave it to someone else simply because she assumed our family could not have afforded the camera Kevin had used and therefore it was a stolen camera.

As a young boy, Kevin had worked hard to earn the money to buy the camera. The teacher's stole from Kevin an award that meant so much to him and humiliated him as well. I wonder what she would think had she known how hard Kevin worked to make for a better life for his family. If she had seen him as a child running so fast to capture a rabbit—hoping to provide food for our family—and his disappointment when the rabbit escaped his grasp when running beneath a barb-wire fence. It is an example of the prejudice and discrimination that happens when people in positions of leadership become lazy in their thinking and do not seek to educate themselves.

Kevin became rebellious and difficult to discipline at school. Was it due to the way he was repeatedly treated by teachers and staff? He was ready to fight anyone at the drop of a hat. He had a good heart, even as confused and angry as he was. Many of my brothers ended up on a similar path given the terrible treatment we received from teachers.

When Kevin was older, he built a car using parts of other damaged vehicles from a salvage, or "junk," yard. Other guys of his age laughed and mocked his efforts, shaming him. It was brutal for him. Yet, none of those spoiled young men could have done what he accomplished. Most of their cars and privileges were paid for by their parents. Kevin did not have an easy life; it is amazing that he kept going on, working, and making his way in life.

Is it any wonder that many of my siblings quit school and did not continue seeking a higher education at that time? School was extremely difficult for us who were "underprivileged." Thank God that more help is now available for impoverished people, though there is more work to be done.

We children were blessed that Mama taught us how to think and encouraged us to learn. Admirably, many of my siblings engaged in more education later in life. They are all extremely intelligent and capable people with tremendous potential and who built careers for themselves.

Grandma and Harold

Grandma Miller, Daddy's mother, lived several miles from our house. I saw Grandma Miller so few times that I hardly could recognize her. My sister, Breanne, said Grandma was a decent and good woman.

Grandma Miller also had a daughter that I didn't know about until later in life. One time this daughter was so angry that Grandma Miller bought my Mama a new coat, that she cut it into pieces.

And there was Harold.

Grandma Miller set a precedent for those days because she never went anywhere without her son Harold, Daddy's half-brother. Harold was "mentally handicapped." In those days, if someone in the family was mentally or physically "handicapped," they would be placed in some sort of institution and usually never seen again. But Grandma didn't put Harold "away." Grandma wasn't ashamed of Harold, and when you saw her, you saw Harold.

I was told my uncle Harold had only the mentality of a twelve-year old, but he seemed smart to me. He was sweet and kind and interesting when he spoke. He loved assembling model airplanes. He hung some of them from the ceiling in his tidy bed-room and would place others around the perimeter of his room.

I remember vividly the day I was walking home from school with a friend who was drinking a bottle of soda. I wasn't sure at first, but I thought it was Grandma and Harold walking toward us on the sidewalk in front of the block of small stores lined up beside each other near the courthouse. As we drew closer, I realized it was Grandma. When she saw that my friend had a soda, Grandma took me into one of the small shops and bought me a soda so that I could have one too. I was so thrilled and astounded! I never forgot her kindness.

Once, at Grandma's house, I asked her why she was putting a sprig of greenery in a small, white, porcelain pan of water she was warming on the stove. She said it was alfalfa for her to drink for her arthritis.

Grandma lived closer to town than we did when we lived on North Walnut. Her neat little house with a screened-in porch was several blocks across town near the cemetery. She had to walk a distance south, then a block west, and cross the railroad tracks, and then walk northward, a mile or two from there to come to our house.

The crossing at the railroad tracks were where, many years later, my good friend and some of her friends were killed when their car was hit by a train going south; behind it on the other track was a train going north. They didn't see the North-bound train, and they were all killed. I lost a good friend and quietly carried that grief for many years.

As a young girl, that railroad was the only time I ever got to spend with Daddy. Daddy gave me some wheat stems that stuck from the bottom of a rail car that was parked and showed me how to chew the grain like gum. That was a special and momentous time for me.

Grandma Miller was unique and brave in refusing to put Harold "away." Especially when society was embarrassed by anyone with "peculiarities" regardless of whether they were mental or physical, including women experiencing hormonal issues. In my adult years, a woman who managed a vitamin shop told me something that happened in her family. This tragic story happened to many women over many, many years.

Her grandmother was placed in an asylum when she experienced many effects of premenstrual syndrome, commonly referred to as PMS today. Of course, in those days, no one would acknowledge that such a thing existed. Women with PMS would be diagnosed as mentally ill and subjected to horrible treatments or confined to institutions. Thankfully, eventually, a woman doctor experiencing PMS began to research and speak out. Still, even today it irritates some people who deny such a medical situation exists.

When I grew up, and after I married Trent, I knew about premenstrual syndrome (PMS) long before the medical society acknowledged it. I had researched the issue for years, having experienced it personally. No woman I knew at the time would discuss it, much less admit to having any issues.

I found help for myself at a vitamin shop who had not heard of PMS. However, they were astute and suggested we break down my symptoms and find a vitamin for each one. I don't remember some of the herbs, except for Dong Quai, but they totally changed my problem—and my life. And I only experienced symptoms once a month. Later, when some of my women friends became courageous enough to admit they experienced PMS, I sadly discovered that one of them had to contend with symptoms three weeks out of a month. Thank God that there is now help for women. Tragically, there is no way to know how many women over the many years were divorced or placed in institutions because of the complications of a now recognized hormonal problem!

Grandma took care of Harold throughout her life until her other family forced her into a nursing home when she was older. To us, it was a tragedy, but we had no say in the matter; Daddy's stepbrothers and stepsisters had the authority to make the decisions. Mama always cared about Grandma Miller, and I would go with her to the nursing home to visit Grandma. Grandma would tell us that people were stealing the food we took to her, but there was little we could do. She lost weight so fast that she did not live long.

Christmas to Remember

Mama made magic on Christmas! One year all I wanted was a pair of spurs, and at Christmas I was thrilled to get a little tin pair to put over the back of my shoes!

In 1945, Germany surrendered to the United States military followed by the surrender of Japan two months later. We were children of the post-war era, and the Navy still maintained bases of military installations around the country, one of which was located near our town. Personnel from the base and soldiers in white uniforms were commonly seen in our town. In those days people were taught honor and decency and most of the soldiers were considerate and had good character. They were also held to strict standards by their naval officers, which is to be commended. Still, with so many soldiers around, Daddy would always walk my oldest sister home from work each night, as she had taken on a job at the movie theater in town.

One winter day we were surprised when some soldiers, dressed in immaculate dark blue navy suits, came to our house, and politely invited some of us children to attend the special upcoming Christmas celebration! We were in awe and extremely impressed that these military men, so elegantly attired and so courteous, would come to our house to invite us to a special Christmas dinner. They had decided to host a special Christmas dinner for impoverished children living in the area. I wished Mama had been invited—she deserved to be—but the dinner was for children.

Mama felt comfortable allowing us children to go to the Christmas dinner at the Naval Station since the soldiers were held to exacting standards. She accepted the soldiers' invitation and gave us permission to go. We children were ecstatic.

The day couldn't come soon enough for us. When the day came, Rachel and I dressed as lovely as we could and carefully styled our hair. I don't recall how many of us children went.

In the early evening, the soldiers arrived at our home to pick us up. They came to our door, dressed in their immaculate dark blue uniform, and escorted each of us to the spotless, shiny car. They were so polite and considerate—Rachel and I felt like princesses!

Our chaperones attempted to make us comfortable. I was incredibly nervous, shy, and quiet but I tried to answer questions politely. Everything was more than we were accustomed to. We were escorted into the dinner room; it was so beautiful with long tables covered in crisp, white tablecloths, and sparkling vases with bouquets of colorful flowers. The aroma of food, wafting from the kitchen, was incredible. My stomach rumbled embarrassingly with impatience.

At each table, the silverware was polished, gleaming, and precisely placed at each setting. Such beauty made one want to sit up straight; it felt amazing to be a part of this elaborate party.

A large Christmas tree with sparkling lights added a warm glow to the room, and Christmas decorations adorned the tables and walls. The ball room was exquisite and exciting—they had done so much work! Why would they do this for us?

Our smiling, dignified hosts served us plates overflowing with an amazing array of healthy cuisine still steaming with warmth. The food was delicious—to this day I remember the smell of the gravy at that marvelous dinner and the memory returns when I smell a certain brown gravy. They even served us dessert! We were so thrilled to be part of the festivities; the generosity and incredible experience was so meaningful to us.

When the soldiers took us home, they opened our doors for us and walked us to the door. They treated Mama with such respect, and that meant the world to me.

Years later my oldest brother, Randall, joined the Navy. He proudly served our country, and then became an architect. My younger brother joined the army after high school and proudly served his country.

God, help me to be so kind, and bless all those men and women who made such an effort to make our lives so special. Their generosity made my life better and made me feel more capable.

Not Letting Go

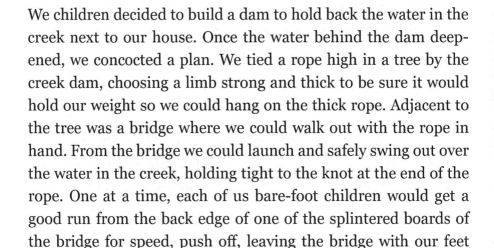

We children decided to build a dam to hold back the water in the creek next to our house. Once the water behind the dam deepened, we concocted a plan. We tied a rope high in a tree by the creek dam, choosing a limb strong and thick to be sure it would hold our weight so we could hang on the thick rope. Adjacent to the tree was a bridge where we could walk out with the rope in hand. From the bridge we could launch and safely swing out over the water in the creek, holding tight to the knot at the end of the rope. One at a time, each of us bare-foot children would get a good run from the back edge of one of the splintered boards of the bridge for speed, push off, leaving the bridge with our feet flying upward to leverage our jump, hanging on tight to the round knot tied at the end of the rope, and rush to let the swing carry us forward, gleefully flying freely while swinging through the air as high and far as we could, then letting go of the rope and bravely dropping into the water with a loud splash.

When it was my turn to swing over the water, I followed the examples of the siblings before me, even tucking the rope between my legs so my arms weren't required to support all my weight. I ran and jumped, pulling my legs and feet upward, to push myself higher and farther. Unfortunately, I forgot to let go and the propulsion caused the rope to swing wildly off course, continuing in an arc that abruptly stopped as my small body collided with the unyielding tree.

The force wrenched the rope from my hands and legs and I fell into the water. Pain radiated from my face to my feet. Where I had wrapped my legs around the rope, my thighs burned like fire from slipping down the coarse rope. I flailed, crying, hoping that someone would come and help me—but no one did. Moaning in agony, I managed to pull myself up the dirt bank and was obliged to sustain my wounds and suffering. Finally I succeeded in returning to the house. I didn't tell Mama; she had impressed on us children that we were to be strong. Eventually the pain lessened, but it tormented me for some time.

A Star of Hope

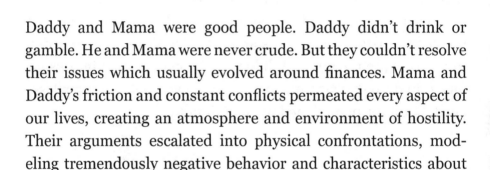

Daddy and Mama were good people. Daddy didn't drink or gamble. He and Mama were never crude. But they couldn't resolve their issues which usually evolved around finances. Mama and Daddy's friction and constant conflicts permeated every aspect of our lives, creating an atmosphere and environment of hostility. Their arguments escalated into physical confrontations, modeling tremendously negative behavior and characteristics about relationships. Although we children became accustomed to this dynamic, the frequent tensions affected us all.

Though still just a small girl, one night I was in deep despair. Sitting in the dark, on the edge of the bed with my sisters asleep, I cried out to God, deeply sad with life. And then, looking up through the window, I saw the star-cross in the Northern sky. I had never seen this sparkling emblem before! I stared, in shock. I knew that God had sent me what must be an angel! Excited, I ran to Mama and Daddy's bed and woke Mama. "I saw an angel!" I told her breathlessly.

Sleepily, Mama mumbled, "Go say, Speak Lord, thy servant heareth." I ran back into my bedroom, and looking up at the brilliant figure, I repeated what Mama had told me to say. Silently, begging in my heart, I longed to hear the "angel" speak. "Stay, stay" I pleaded with the glowing form, but to my dismay, very slowly it receded into the darkness of the night sky. I was disappointed yet thrilled because I knew God had spoken to me through this brilliantly glowing image. That belief would carry me through coming years of sorrow and anguish.

Mama and Daddy had a fight one night, and Mama, upset, went out the door and said she was never coming back. I believed her, and climbed upon a wooden chair, broken-hearted. The immense depth of sorrow I felt was unbearable. Tears fell like Niagara Falls and my soul was seriously wounded.

In the darkness, I could see the red ashes of Daddy's cigarette across the room, but I could not see him. I cried and cried and cried, the little girl that I was, sitting on that stiff, wooden-backed chair, thinking I would never see Mama again. I was devastated, trembling as every tear fell. Sobbing and choking, anguish tight in my chest.

It was like heaven opened when, after an eternity, the front door opened quietly and Mama entered the dark room. I carried a dreadful wound that only healed years later when God knitted my heart back together.

Sometimes, when she thought no one could see her, Mama would cry with deep, throbbing sobs—and then she would wipe her red-rimmed, swollen eyes with her apron so no one would know that she had cried. Then she would hastily get up and go back to her back-breaking work for the constant needs of her large family.

Even so, my imagination of the future didn't remotely consider the painful realities yet to come.

We children became used to our parents' constant fighting, but it was detrimental for all of us. We were not allowed to intervene in our parents' struggles and Mama discouraged us children from interacting with Daddy. It was heart-breaking to us, and we responded by masking our emotions with silence and burying our thoughts. As children, our attitudes, and interactions with each other were also damaged. We each developed different patterns, with some siblings becoming outwardly aggressive while others of us drew inward. Even in a family of so many people living in a modest space, we often felt isolated and alone.

A Star of Hope

I heard you crying, Mama, when times were very bad
With apron, wipe those tears away so we would not be sad
I saw you making gravy, using water 'stead of milk
And felt you brush my tangled hair until it felt like silk
I saw you push the buggy, and try to get our books
I saw you lift your chin up high, when we all got "those looks."
I saw you wash those clothes by hand
From morning until night
I saw you scrub and iron and patch
Sometimes 'til it grew light.
I saw you coming through the rain
And chilled to very bone,
You placed a coat around me
And led me safely home.
How did you sing? I'll never know
But how it soothed my mind.
How stayed you those appalling years,
So patient, strong, and kind?
You had twelve little babies
With courage gave each birth—
I think you are the greatest mom
Whoever walked on earth.

Milk and Cookies

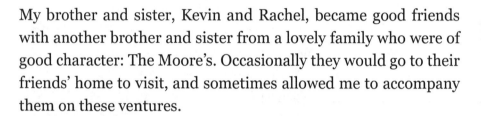

My brother and sister, Kevin and Rachel, became good friends with another brother and sister from a lovely family who were of good character: The Moore's. Occasionally they would go to their friends' home to visit, and sometimes allowed me to accompany them on these ventures.

I was quick to accept their invitation; I enjoyed the company of the Moore's. Usually, I was the only one who wanted to tag along. My other siblings didn't want to walk that far; the Moore's house was out in the country and was a considerable distance. The path to their house was the railroad track because the surrounding landscape was overgrown pasture—almost like wilderness. It always seemed slightly scary with its miles of dense brush, brambly weeds, trees, and who-knows-what critters?

The only other life between our house and their farm was wildlife. Hawks hovered in the sky before dropping in a blur of speed to attack unaware and unsuspecting prey. Rabbits scurried about cautiously, but were still the frequent victims of hawks, sneaky coyotes, and bold red foxes. Skunks and snakes hid in unpredictable places.

The railroad track presented its own challenges. There was always the chance that a train might come rumbling like a monster down the track; when that happened, you had to quickly find a safe place to take cover as the powerful monster roared by, its thick, black smoke billowing from the chimney perched on top of the locomotive. Sometimes the passing train seemed eternal; train car after train car rumbling down the tracks, being pulled by the scary, loud, vibrating, monstrous, immensely powerful, and noisy engine. Especially scary was the rapid approach of a train while you were walking a trestle above a deep ravine; you had little time to run to the embankment opposite the oncoming train and jump aside. When a train passed, the wind it created was breathtaking, shaking you a little.

The pastures we walked by looked as if they had not held cows or horses for many years; they were overgrown with fibrous, entangled brush and weeds. Eventually we would arrive at the Moore's.

Mr. and Mrs. Moore were lovely, kind people and their love for their two children was very apparent. Mrs. Moore was a kind and gentle spirit, and always kept their small home very neat and cheerful and friendly. In the kitchen was a shiny, white, porcelain, wood-burning kitchen stove. The shiny white, glossy, surface was so gleaming and slick, I wanted to touch it and glide my finger over it. The stove had no nicks, no stains from use—I had never seen such a pristine stove. Above the spotless surface were dainty, veiled, frilly curtains, neatly pulled back and tied with a colorful ribbon.

We children were accustomed to the obvious stares from so many people regarding our appearance, but the Moore's took no apparent notice of the clothes we wore. Our feet were as tough as leather from not wearing shoes; for us, shoes were hard to come by. Most of them didn't fit anyway, and we had to put cardboard in the bottoms to cover the holes in the soles.

With few means, Mama continuously had the difficult challenge of keeping us growing children dressed in ample clothes. Mama was proud; I observed her embarrassment on the rare occasions someone would bring bags of clothes to our house. Most of the donated dresses went to my older sisters. Once, at school in the coat room, a young girl with golden curls looked at the dress I was wearing, pointed at it, and said my dress was exactly like one she once had. I knew it was a charity dress, and I took offense, feeling disconcerted. But my reaction wasn't fair to her because she meant it very innocently. The Moore's never seemed to be concerned about such things, they were just authentically kind and good.

Mr. Moore allowed us children to ride their horses. I was so excited, but the horse I rode was not as thrilled and surreptitiously navigated towards a rather concealed wire, stretched horizontally. I didn't see the wire as the horse darted below the wire, which caught me off guard and knocked me off the horse.

THE WIRE KNOCKED ME OFF THE HORSE.

Mr. Moore was immensely proud of his large flock of white turkeys. He was a quiet soul, not given to much expression, but his eyes lit up and his pale cheeks brightened as he told us how he hand-raised the turkeys and how important they were for their family's financial future. We children listened with sincere interest and hoped his arduous work would reimburse his efforts and provide great profit for them.

Then, this particularly remarkable day became even more amazing! Mrs. Moore told us kids that if we would collect and carry the wood into the house, she would bake cookies for us!

We couldn't believe our good luck and all of us scurried about quickly to gather the wood and carry it carefully into the kitchen to stack it neatly into the wood box. Mrs. Moore wasted no time fulfilling her promise. We children were so excited as we stood quietly and observed. From the cupboard, she retrieved a bag of white flour and other needed ingredients. She mixed sugar and eggs in a bowl and began to measure each additional ingredient before placing in the bowl. She fluttered about, mixed the ingredients with her pale, delicate hands. We were astonished that she could construct the dough so fast. She placed more wood into the stove, to warm the oven, and then plumped out the opulent, fluffy dough onto the lightly floured table, smoothed it with her floured fingers, took a rolling pin, floured it, then began to roll out the dough in a measured, even, round pattern. Then came the cookie cutter, oval, with a metal handle, and sharp metallic cutting edge. She began to cut matching ovals, like tiny moons, and replacing the trimmings back into a ball that she rolled and pressed and sculpted back into reusable dough. She rolled it out just as she had done before, cut it into sharp, oval, delightful shapes and carefully place each shape onto the greased pan. What an exciting time we had that day.

We children were so enthusiastic. However, we behaved politely as Mama had carefully taught us. Mrs. Moore slid the pan of the neatly cut ovals into the oven and we waited—it seemed for a century. When the oven door was opened, the aroma was overwhelming!

Mrs. Moore used a cloth to grip the pans and set them on the table. But then, to add to our unexpected treasure, Mrs. Moore took another lovely dish with a fragile, pastel lid of soft flowers, from the cabinet shelf and sprinkled a sparkling dust of sugar over the aromatic, crisp, cookies!

It was unbelievable. Aware of our impatience and barely bridled enthusiasm, the beautiful, golden-brown goodies were barely cool when she offered them to us. We were courteous, but ecstatic. Gobbling cookies, especially such succulent ones, was something we had not expected. We were thrilled.

The sweetness of the delicate sugar cookies rolled around our tongues and even the minute crumbs danced with joy as we chewed them. We rubbed our tongues against every morsel until not even a tiny taste could be found. We seldom had such luxurious treats to eat as we couldn't afford cookies in our home.

I have never forgotten the cookies, or Mr. and Mrs. Moore's kindness and generosity. A cup of cold water given in Jesus' name will be rewarded.

In the latter part of the afternoon, my brother and sister began to prepare for the return home, knowing we needed ample time for the return journey before the sun set on this wonderful, incredible day. Our hearts full, we children thanked the Moore's as we had been taught to do.

The Storm

I was reluctant to leave this moment with the Moore's. I began the journey homeward leisurely, soon trailing my brother and sister. They paused to wait, and when I approached them, Kevin warned me to hurry and keep up with him and Rachel.

Seeing my reticence, Rachel sighed impatiently, her mouth tightened, and with a parting remark, hesitated, then departed impatiently, deciding to head on down the tracks without waiting for me. Kevin, his furrowed brows showing his annoyance with my nonchalant attitude, attempted to severely warn, compel, and convince me to come with them. Stop dawdling!

He persisted for some time to reason with and cajole me. When apparent that that I wasn't going to be diverted from my determined reluctance and bland defiance, he accepted that I wasn't going to be convinced by his advice and aggressive arguments. With his admonitions having no visible effect, he ceased his worthy efforts, and headed down the railroad tracks, hoping his contrary sister would respond to his abandonment. I continued my leisurely pace as he slowly vanished into the distance, increasing his pace to catch up with my sister before she disappeared on the horizon.

I mumbled some appeasements to myself, and casually walked along, lingering along the path to examine and gather all the allurements of nature. Rachel and Kevin had disappeared down the railroad tracks on the path to home. Even though I was isolated in a wild countryside, I wasn't concerned by their absence. I was used to being out in nature. Butterflies flitted, their multifaceted tints shimmering in wispy movements. Wildflowers greeted me and beckoned me to investigate their complex formations and scents. The little rocks between the thick-hued, rough, wooden ties between the iron rails, when inspected more closely, were as individual in size, shape, and hues as the people that God created. I continued my explorations, watching pink-breasted robins and temperamental blue-jays and red-headed woodpeckers pecking on the bark of trees. My only distant concern was vaguely listening for the sound of a train engine rumbling down the rail.

The movements of birds and butterflies abated as the silence of dark clouds emerged. I had failed to notice change in atmosphere and the goosebumps on my chilled body. I shivered as a shadow rolled over the sky and the wind became noticeable. My hair began to blow annoyingly across my face and whip at my clothes. Then, I felt the earth shake and vibrate beneath my feet. Suddenly fearful, I thought a massive engine was coming down the track.

But no locomotive appeared. I gazed upward, witnessing the sky melting into darkness. The looming clouds thickened and ominously stretched across the sky. Thunder rattled the earth under my feet. My brother and sister were out of sight, far ahead of me with too much distance to hear my calling out to them.

Suddenly, the velocity and ferocity of the storm encircled me. Branches were ripped from bushes and trees. The gravel and wooden rails that I was depending on to guide me were becoming submerged in the rising waters. In just moments, the path home became hidden beneath broken limbs and debris.

I feared the demonic turbulence would tear away my dress, rip off my hair and knock me off the rails. I was terrified that I would fall from the rails and be tossed into a crevice. Rain blew sideways, filling every ravine and gully with water, leaving no place for refuge. My thin, cotton dress was so drenched that the pouring water flowing off the thin, torn fabric was like a whip against my legs. The small shiny pebbles I had wistfully collected spilled from my pockets. The bouquet of the wildflowers that I had gathered for Mama were ripped from my rigidly clasped hand, petals flying wildly in all directions as the lightening flashed.

All hell had broken loose, and hell has no mercy!

By sheer muscular effort, my seven-year-old body fought the storm's onslaught. My clothing was drenched and plastered with debris. My eyes were burning from the constant needles of the belligerent rain. Debris pounded my face until it bled. My hair was plastered to my scalp, with the long ends repeatedly striking my face. Moving forward required all my strength and I desperately tried to find any resemblance of a path along the tracks that might lead toward home.

The shrieking wind pummeled me backwards. I didn't know what danger lay beneath or beside the slope of the tracks; there was no place to seek shelter. I could not see my hand though I held it before my eyes. I could not determine where I was as the darkness, like a cloak of malice, engulfed the world about me. The only flicker of light was when the lightning exploded, and for a brief second, I would attempt to assess where I was.

The sky crackled with brilliant webs of electricity as lightning thrashed. The crescendo of thunder shook the earth like thousands of chariots racing to war. My arms reached outward, trying to keep my balance, as I tried to feel the railroad planks beneath my feet. It was as if all hell was swirling around me-pushing, pulling, striking, blinding me. The enemy of my soul, the one I had prayed against for many years, was going to destroy me!

"Jesus, I need you," I cried with lips trembling. If only I had obeyed my wiser brother. I felt a paroxysm of weeping, but what good was it now?

My cries were lost in the shrill of the storm and the explosive thunder. No one could have heard my cries in the turbulence. Then, a flash of lightening permitted me to see vague shadows ahead and my heart sank with more fear! I had fought so hard only to realize I had gone too far! I was lost and needed to turn around and go back!

In utter despair, lost, wounded, overwhelmed with fear, terrified and desperate for my life, I cried out to my God—the Great God of the universe! Then a long tail of lightning illuminated the sheen of wet rain on an iron rail. I raised my foot to step over that rail...

Suddenly, a welcoming golden light enveloped me in a mantle of warmth. I was motionless as the glowing light penetrated my soul. I stood at the open door of my home, my mother's silhouette slowly revealing her eyes staring in shock at the bedraggled, drenched, bleeding and torn figure before her. She awoke to the reality that it was me standing there, and I was quickly hustled into the bedroom. Mama removed my soaked and tattered clothes and placed me in bed, covering me

THE STORM WAS MERCILESS!

with warm blankets. Then she brought me hot tomato soup in a thick cup. Such tender care I had never remembered.

No one had come to look for me. In the bustle of many energetic children, the lack of my presence was unnoticed. They could understand how I had gotten home in the storm, with the creek flooding and the path lost in the torrents of water and debris.

But I knew. I had been in the grip of the enemy, Satan. Then I was at the door of home, the bright, golden light holding me, comforting my soul with its blanket of salvation. To this day, I believe an angel of God picked up this little girl who had prayed daily to God and carried me home.

The devil tried to destroy me with the horrific storm, but Jesus intervened, just as He has so many times to help us all. He doesn't see our stature, our wealth, our poverty; he doesn't concern himself with our traditions. He only wants to save our souls and offer the hope of a full life.

Just as I chose to ignore the words and warnings of my brother that momentous day, how foolish and ignorant we humans can be, ignoring the truth found in the scriptures—teaching us of the difficult and dangerous outcomes that occur when we ignore God's wise council. The propensity of modern culture is to consider the thinking of older generations as outdated and irrelevant. Yet, God is never outdated and never will be. I survived to tell this experience because of His grace and mercy, and am thankful for the angels that protect us even at times when we veer from God's path for us.

In the Deep

Mama was an excellent swimmer and would take her children swimming when she found country bodies of water. One day Mama and Daddy took us swimming at a place in the country called "Craigs." Mama directed me and all the young children who could not swim to stay in the shallow, rocky area to play and, if we chose, to look for crawdads and fat tadpoles, which was always a challenge and much fun. Tadpoles grow legs and one day morph into frogs. To find crawdads, it was important to have a container handy, if you planned on collecting them. Normally, the best way to accomplish catching a crawdad, was to wait quietly and be still, waiting until a crawdad, feeling safe, would creep out from under a rock, look around, and feeling safe when nothing was moving, scurry from under the rock. Then, if you were quick enough, you could compose your fingers to grab the crawdad on its soft back. If you knew to grasp its back, and avoid its pinchers, many times you achieved success. Then there was a sense of pleasure in dropping the crawdad into your waiting container.

Catching crawdads was a challenge, and searching for the large ones was even more challenging because they were more wary, and their pinchers could be very painful. I enjoyed the time spent searching and capturing the little worthy, sneaky, and extremely fast opponents. The secret was to out-wait them, then when one emerged from under a rock, you had to quickly grab them. If the crawdads saw you, they would curve their tails under their abdomens and swiftly zip backwards in this position, fleeing back under the rock into their dark hiding place. Another trick they had was to throw up a dirt screen so you could not see them as they disappeared. Catching the little critters was quite an art.

After a time spent chasing and catching them, I compromised Mama's warnings about what area of the water to stay in—and she was adamant about the boundaries that we were allowed to reach, but we were to attempt going no further. The water beyond that rocky distance was very dark and very deep. There was a high cliff over the deep water, and the older swimmers dived from that cliff and swam in the deeper pool.

Like a foolish child, after tiring of chasing slimy, green tadpoles and crusty orange or pink, squishy-shelled crawdads, I pushed the limits, my bare feet feeling all the strangely shaped rocks wet and cold with the shallow water that flowed over their tops and bubbled between their variegated shapes and shadowy edges, ringing around them like soapy lace. Some of the rocks were sharp, some of them smooth, some of them were etched with markings by something, and some even held old shells and ancient fossils and objects that looked like petrified wood.

But later, feeling bored and drawn by curiosity, I meandered toward the rim of the deeper pool. I began stretching my legs over the ridges of wet rock, bending my toes over the rocks at the boundary edge. I was used to physical activity and overrated my strength and underrated the reality of nature's powerful possibilities. Suddenly, my feet would not grip the extraordinarily slimy rocks, no matter how hard I tried to right myself. Too late— my feet began to slip and as I felt my leverage weaken. I realized I was no longer able to balance myself as I swayed back and forth in a final effort to stabilize myself, but to no avail. I was sliding from the slippery rock, like sliding on ice with no ability to stop. Abruptly, I fell from the glass-like, mossy rock into the deep, dark pool of forbidden water.

The deep, dark pool was cold. The depth of the water quickly engulfed me as I sank, and I was trapped in what seemed an eternal sea as black as coal. I flailed, unable to see anything as I held my breath—cheeks round and lips pursed tight to keep the water out of my mouth and lungs.

I struggled against the moving water, fighting my way to the surface for a brief moment to gasp for air and then hopelessly choking as water mixed with air filled my lungs. Unable to call for help as I choked, I flung about my arms and legs, but panic only hastened the impending danger surrounding me. I had heard that if a person goes under the water three times, they will not come back up—they will drown. I surfaced again and tried to scream, but water splashed into my face and I knew I was going back down. I tried to gulp in air, but water flooded my mouth. I tried to swallow the invading water as I sealed my mouth, holding my breath while my lungs were forcefully begging for air. The dark, frigid water enveloped me as my body sank mercilessly again.

Down, down, down into the cold blackness of death. No one seemed to notice that I was drowning; people were actively engaged in enjoying the beautiful, fun, sunshiny day. God help me! I cried. I was once again able to fight my way upwards, and I knew that when I reached the surface this time, it was my last chance at life. As the sun hit my face and fleeting light touched my eyes, all splashing water about me inhibited any sound from my throat, I gulped in more water, cutting off my breath. I had drawn no one's attention and my body began sinking for the third time.

The black water drew me down, down...

AND I knew

I couldn't

make it

back up

again.

My spirits had soared momentarily each time I had been pushed to the surface, but each time had been shattered as the splashing had prevented any cry for help. My fate seemed sealed, and the darkness was desolate; I was totally alone in this horrible ordeal. Alone to die in this dark, cold, hell. Alone is hell. Please, God, help me.

And then, at that fateful moment, I felt a slight tug. Rachel, not even paying much attention, caught my double-capped blouse sleeve and without any noticeable emotion, as if it were a mere, normal move, indolently pulled my blouse sleeve toward the shallows where she was involved in something of interest that held her attention. She didn't even know I was drowning. Ironically, she was unconscious of my perilous plight.

She lacked any expression of concern as I tried to speak my gratitude, but I couldn't breathe to tell her. In great pain, overwhelmed, I lay on the rocks, gasping desperately for air. My lungs were in enormous pain.

I was so grateful, I wanted to tell her so badly that she had saved my life. I persisted but I couldn't talk and was too weak and had no strength. She was nonchalant, only remotely really believing what I was making such an effort to say. One of the saddest things of our childhood is that we weren't taught to show any affection.

Engulfed in my painful predicament, I heard shouting and saw the adults' pantomiming gestures at the top of the cliff. Daddy's friend was jumping about wildly as he attempted to pull a pant leg off his leg to remove his pants, but Mama didn't wait. She ran and dived from the high, rocky cliff.

A huge circle of water rose into the air as Mama's body broke the surface of deep water. My little brother, Stephen, was bobbing up and down in the dark waters, his skin so blue and black that I faintly recognized him. He, too, had slipped into the deep pool of water and had held his breath so long that his face was blue-black. Mama grasped him and swam him to land, saving his life.

Nobody but Jesus and I knew that I had almost drowned a few minutes before. After I had regained some strength, I attempted to explain to Rachel that I had almost drowned, emphasizing that she had rescued me, and I was so grateful. No matter how I insisted, she didn't seem to take me seriously.

Many years later, when we were adults, I sent Rachel a set of ruby red jewelry to thank her for saving my life.

California Dreamin'

Mama and Daddy traveled frequently. They could pack so fast, we children hardly noticed until we were on the road. I don't know if they both wanted to travel—I suppose they did. One day they packed up the car and put all of us children into the back seat. The North Walnut house was now history, and we were off to California, and then later to Oregon. Like so many people in those days, Daddy and Momma kept looking for a better life.

So many people were displaced, distraught, looking for jobs, homes, health, and thank God that the president of the time had the courage to stand against powerful and wealthy corporations and uncompassionate groups that had no empathy for the poor people. Never mind the damage done to people by the wars, the plague, the dust bowl, the depression, the horrid conditions of some jobs, such as mining, the lack of finances for people to help themselves.

One night we stopped for gas at a small gas station someplace between Kansas and California. It was a very dark night, and scary when a uniformed police officer approached our car and shined his bright flashlight into our car while Daddy was in the station building.

We children shivered nervously with concern, not having any experience with policemen. The policeman left, and then returned to our dismay. Our apprehension turned into surprise as the police officer handed us two large paper bags of food through the open windows. Then, he was gone into the darkness, not even waiting for any vocalization of gratitude. God bless that kind man; we really needed that food.

When we got to California, we had another God-blessed, fascinating, and memorable experience. Daddy got lost and pulled over. He parked our two-seated car packed with children and left to go find information about our directions and destination.

Mama and we children noticed we had parked close to an outdoor saloon. We had never seen one before, and next door to the outdoor bar, surrounded by men, were tall buildings, one of which had a sign that offered baths for about a nickel.

The outdoor bar was filled with all sorts of men in all stages of sobriety—or not. Some of the individuals were dirty, messy, and unkempt, indulging on the sweltering day from mugs containing some liquid—I can only guess. Some of the men were singing and seemed to be enjoying themselves and each other in loud conversation. They seemed startled when they saw our car there, especially with about ten children's eyes watching them curiously and intently, including Mama's gaze.

Seeing our staring faces, they recognized not only our barefaced curiosity, but also our sweating, pink faces. Our thirst and hunger revealed itself in our tired, crowded bodies. Surprisingly, those drunken, disheveled, stumbling men, seemed to sober up as they examined us with squinty eyes.

There was some mild commotion, and then to our disbelief, these men began to carry mugs to our car, Considerately, they handed Mama and each of us children a full mug of cold root beer. We were shocked, but as soon as Mama nodded her approval, we did not hesitate to drink the cold, sweet, honey-like liquid that danced in our mouths and rolled down our dry throats like a thirst-quenching amber.

We were immensely grateful, and a little confused. How could these derelict men be so generous when others were so unkind? They were so compassionate and made no gestures to suggest any evil intentions. The area is still known by its infamous and scornfully title "Skid-Row."

Daddy returned with correct directions and on we went. On the way, we picked strawberries in a large field for a while. Sometimes I would choose to eat the red, ripe, fruit instead of placing it into my basket.

We went to Grandma Holland's for a few days, but not long. It wasn't a pleasant interaction. I felt like she didn't want us there; she couldn't care of all our family and hers. She did advise us children to never admit to having any "Indian blood." However, kids at school frequently told me that I looked "Indian" because of my high cheekbones. I came to not care; it seemed so shallow to depend on the assessment of others for your sense of self-worth.

The next leg of the trip was to Uncle Bud's in Oregon. We tried to hire out to cut weeds from some vegetable field, but that didn't last long either.

Uncle Bud had some prize-winning milk cows and an extremely dangerous bull that he kept in a thickly wooded pen.

He allowed me to go to the cheese factory with him, riding in his pick-up truck, where he sold his rich milk for cheese. I found it fascinating to see all the yellow rounds of cheese being cooled in special rooms.

He wanted some of us children to stay there with him, but we weren't interested and refused his offer, courteously, not wanting to be separated from our family. We thought he was a little creepy too. I hope he is now in heaven, enjoying God's presence.

Before long, we returned to Kansas and another house. I was eight years old.

Sweet Memories

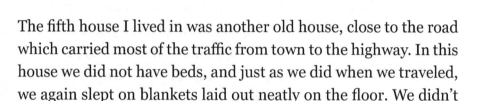

The fifth house I lived in was another old house, close to the road which carried most of the traffic from town to the highway. In this house we did not have beds, and just as we did when we traveled, we again slept on blankets laid out neatly on the floor. We didn't live in this house for long.

I didn't really like this house. Why did we have to move there? It was so close to the busy road that ran through town. But I had learned that where we went, we just went. There was never an explanation.

Mama made every effort to run an organized and wholesome household, but without dependable finances, it was extremely difficult. But she always maintained her morals, decency, and honor.

We children tried to help Mama. Kevin would cut cane poles and take us fishing to catch fish for our meals. We climbed every nut tree we found. We were delighted to discover walnut trees near this old house. We climbed the trees to harvest the ripened walnuts, their round, green husks covering the oval-shaped shell that contained the delicate and sweet meats. It was a demanding pursuit that required us to ignore the clinging green and brown stains that liberally soaked into the skin and refused to relinquish its dye no matter how zealously we scrubbed with wet, soapy cloths. Still, the sticky stains that soaked in so determinedly didn't prevent our escapades for free food.

Surprisingly, there is medicinal benefit in the tough, rough, bumpy, green outer cover. If its greenish-black dye is placed on a ringworm, it can heal the problem. I did that once when Mama told me to use the inner dye of the green hull, and very soon the red ring worm was gone.

We children spent hours searching for rocks or bricks or old forgotten hammers—any tool capable of harvesting the meat of the nut. The first step was to split apart the thick green outer covering, revealing the hard, wooden shell. Beating open the hard shells of walnuts required a resolute spirit. As hungry children, we engaged in this tedious and complex effort for the satisfying reward of a tasty morsel.

This procedure had to be done with care and finesse. If you occasionally accomplished the task of splitting the two sections of the shell without pulverizing the meat, it was a moment of worthy recognition of superior skill. Invariably, some of the pieces would be smashed beyond retrieval.

The highest reward was collecting the whole pieces of the nut's meat! This achievement was envied, as the whole nut meats, then delicately picked out of the shell were large enough to offer a triumph of the sweet, rich pleasure of taste! This triumph was delicious, but difficult to repeat.

Some of us became proficient after numberless attempts to redeem whole "halves." Cracking the shell into irregular pieces warranted that it was going to be a tedious and lengthy procedure picking out the tiny pieces of the nut meat.

Another futile struggle was a contender for the patience award. When a nut meat is cracked open, the sheller, especially jubilant if a whole morsel results, is momentarily ignited with fervor, immediately tossing the nut meat into a mouth that is prepared to be immersed in sweet, walnut flavor.

Sometimes this expectation was met with great disillusionment, as the nut meat had degraded and was spoiled, sour, or shriveled. These scurrilous nuts lay in wait for the unsuspecting picker, their unsavory flavor contrasting harshly with their healthy, sweet-tasting counterparts. Eventually, with experience we became more adept at recognizing the scandalous nuts. Thank God for prolific nut trees with all their health benefits—they were a valuable resource of nourishment to our diet.

Mulberry trees were another benefit to our health. We scaled the trees, quickly recognizing their shiny leaves from a distance. The purple dyes stained our mouths and hands as we gobbled down the berries, but that didn't faze us. We plucked the sweet, ripe berries by the hand-full and without hesitation scooped them into our mouths.

Lithe and experienced, we climbed from limb to limb to reach and consume the berries, When the branches were emptied and the berry supply was exhausted, descended the tree carefully as to not inflict damage to the tree. Mama had also taught us to respect our natural environment that God had created for the benefit of all.

One day, while walking home from school with some of my siblings, we found some berry bushes covered with a resplendent and profuse array of vivid, red fruit growing on wild bushes just a few blocks from our house. We sampled the delicious fruit, then excitedly rushed home to report the news of our exceptional discovery. Mama told us that if we collected the berries that she would make a cobbler!

Enthusiastically we ran home found containers and rushed back to the wild berry bushes to collect the ripe, red fruit and fill our buckets and pans. We picked berries with fervor, ignoring the entanglements, and stinging sharp pricks of the branches and thick abandoned, bramble bushes. Tight clumps of undergrowth fought our progress, but there was a great quantity of berries, and we resolved to pick all we could and at length there were few left untouched. At length we concluded to convey our treasure home.

When we returned home, we watched in suspense as Mama with incredible swiftness, mixed a large ball of pie dough, powdered the table with flour, and rolled out three crusts to fit into a deep pan. She stretched and then placed the first oblong piece of dough onto the bottom of the pan, fitting it around the edges with her fingers. She then spooned some of the berries which she had mixed with some white sugar into the pan over the soft, but firm dough. We watched with no small admiration as Mama spliced small pieces of left-over dough into the larger balls. Any remnant disappeared into the whole concoction. Mama never wasted anything. She was very thrifty and taught her children to be likewise.

After the first layer of dough and berries had been neatly smoothed over, Mama gingerly placed a second pliable dough rectangle over the prior shimmering red, juicy contents. We children watched eagerly with glowing faces as Mama's graceful hands leveled the second neatly rolled-out, flexible dough rectangle horizontally and evenly over the surface of the abundant profusion of bright red berries and shiny crimson juice that had been thickened with flour.

The abundant harvest of wild berries we had gathered, with Mama's competent handiwork, was emerging into a composition that drew a long sigh from we anxious onlookers. The delightful spectacle of grandeur encouraged our already salivating appetite! We watched Mama's movements as she fearlessly constructed, fastidiously and completely composed the compilation of the ingredients, her calculations precise as she manipulated all the components of the flour, dough, and berries.

We observed this whole procedure, and I never forgot the experience. I can almost see Mama in her loose, faded dress, her shiny brown hair pinned up in a neat coil, leaning industriously over the white, floured table, with the chipped, thick, bowl, red with the juice of sliced, shiny berries, her paring knife stained with the red juice, a can of lard and a cloth bag of white flour nearby. God bless my dear, amazing mother!

Next, as we children stood around the table watching the sweet concoction take form, Mama ladled more of the sweetened, berry mixture over the rising structure, spreading it thickly over the stretched, ivory-colored, pastry. To our delight, Mama continued to add another eloquent succession of berries and pastry. She scraped the bowl of berries and the thickened juice with a big spoon and deposited it over the middle pastry cunningly suspended the length of the pan, and now colored with blotches of crimson juice. Mama scraped the bowl as clean of berries as possible, to make certain that nothing was left, or wasted. She wanted every drop of the berry mixture to be part of the cobbler.

Mama powdered the table again lightly with flour from the bag and laid out the last ball of dough. She lightly floured the rolling pin and began to roll out the last of the dough. She rolled it with pressure, one way, and then another. She turned it, floured it again lightly, and then rolled it some more, until the whole rectangle of dough was evenly thick, smooth, and floured judiciously so it would not stick to the table.

Then, as we children held our breaths, she lifted the whole delicate structure and slowly covered the second layer of berry mix. We children breathed again as the dough lay over the length and width of the pan. She then pushed and patted the edges of the dough, pinching it against the rim of the pan, fluting the edges of the dough so the berry juiced wouldn't escape. All of this was done with remarkable expertise, finesse, and alacrity.

We children had watched nervously as Mama lifted the remaining slab of flattened dough and cautiously lowered it over the pan, draping it like a pale white blanket, and as she laid it down carefully, positioning it to cover the entire pan. We stared as she then fastened the edges of the dough, pressing it against the sides of the

Excitedly we watched Mama make the berry cobbler!

84

pan with her fingers. The complete process of her meticulous administrations fascinated us.

The necessary interval for the baking of the cobbler profoundly challenged our patience, our tastebuds in a state of craving for an eternity. But then, the rewarding deliciousness was worth every minute of waiting. In the ensuing years, I have always remembered Mama's wonderful succulent cobbler—not just the remarkable taste and not only the recipe that I've never seen repeated, but also the incredible knowledge and morals Mama bestowed on her children with everything that she did!

Loser and Lifesaver

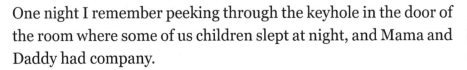

One night I remember peeking through the keyhole in the door of the room where some of us children slept at night, and Mama and Daddy had company.

They were all sitting around the living room on straight-back chairs, talking and laughing. Mama never allowed any risqué language in our home, no matter where we lived. And, for that matter, any place that we visited. She never hesitated to correct any sign of unacceptable language or behavior.

Mama was very principled and moral. Daddy wasn't quite as verbal, but he didn't engage in such antics either, for which I thank God. Mama and Daddy both had fun senses of humor. I wish I had known Daddy better.

The group of grown-ups were drinking sodas! In our household, a rare luxury! Mama and Daddy didn't have an extensive social life. During their conversation, a woman who was somewhat of an acquaintance of Mama asked if she could park her trailer in our yard for a while.

Mama always went the extra mile to excuse people, probably because our own circumstances were always fragile through no fault of her own. Her kind heart made her susceptible to 'losers' asking for help. I say losers because even as a child, I recognized the difference between less fortunate people and losers.

Some people who are poor because of unfortunate circumstances, and then there are those who make a practice of living off other people's labors and kindnesses. Mama didn't necessarily know the difference between losers and the unfortunate; even as a child I seemed to understand that dynamic better than she did.

I did not trust the woman who was appealing to Mama, and my childish intuition would prove to be accurate. Mama allowed the woman, whose name was Mary, to move her house trailer into the side of our yard, and for a while, there wasn't much difficulty.

The house-trailer stayed in our yard, but I couldn't tell if it was inhabited or deserted. Occasionally I saw some movement of people, but seldom. I assumed Mama knew what the irregularities were about. I heard vague remarks and a baby was mentioned. The remarks were muffled and suppressed, it was difficult for me to understand the circumstances and what persuasion she used that caused Mama to grant permission for her move into our yard.

Initially I was confused about the situation, but I accepted that Mama was compassionately helping an acquaintance who had children and a young baby. Whatever calamity Mary had presented to Mama to appeal to Mama's kindness and generosity, and whatever posturing she had suggested, was a baseless performance of pitiful dialogue.

Mary had appealed to Mama's keen sense of decency and mothering, but I noticed the inconsistencies in Mary's stories. However, Mama didn't allow us children to be involved and I was uncertain of what was expected. Mama should have been more open and informative to her children. It wasn't beneficial to us to be uninformed.

Mama seemed to be easily persuaded by Mary's ability to convey distressful news, and the need for emotional dependency. Invariably, Mama's good intentions were being manipulated. She was ambushed because of her compassion for babies and children and the needs of others. It was confusing for me since Mama, who was so moral and required her children to conduct themselves in decent behaviors, was ignoring the questionable, obvious lifestyle of this woman who practically abandoned her role as a mother to enjoy other aspects of life.

It was difficult to believe that Mama was condoning Mary's glaring neglect of her children. Mary would frequently be gone indefinitely, knowing that Mama could not ignore a child in distress. She took advantage of Mama and lived the life of a prodigal mother, abandoning her children for extended periods of time while expecting that Mama would administer whatever necessities the children needed!

Mama but did not seem to comprehend how she was being deceived. I was very apprehensive about the woman, but I suppressed my displeasure since I had no say in the whole matter.

One day Mama was anxious that Mary had been absent for such an extensive period. Surprisingly, she asked me to join her, and we approached the trailer, then knocked on the door.

There was no response, so Mama slowly opened the door, calling out "Hello!" She repeated this several times, as was common courtesy, but no one answered. Slowly we stepped up the sagging steps into the trailer. A sound alerted us, and we turned to witness a grim sight! It was a sight that I never forgot. The room was dismal and cluttered, but our attention was drawn to a small figure lying almost motionless in a baby's bed.

Quickly, we moved to the bed in disbelief. The baby was limp, impassive, and inactive, his eyelids flickered faintly. Very carefully, Mama lifted the weak baby in her arms. We both stared as we saw that one side of the baby's head had been flattened from lying in one position for so long! We were both horrified. Even more appalling, the baby looked like he was about two or three months old, but he was eight months old. He should have been crawling, but he could barely move. It was devastating that this child could have been so neglected and unseen.

Mama held the small boy, wrapped him in a blanket and carried him around, talking to him. She gently rubbed his head, but we were both fearful that the unresponsive child was severely damaged. Every day following, Mama attended to the child, determined to restore him to health. At that time, Mama had birthed and cared for ten babies. She was more skillful and knowledgeable about the care of a baby than anyone else that I ever knew!

Mama worked with the neglected baby each day.

Mama diligently persevered with determination to remedy the tragic plight of the innocent little boy. Her therapy methods consisted of the skill of her fingers and the love in her heart. She was expert in devising strategic aids to employ in accomplishing a goal. Soon he showed several encouraging factors which ignited our hopes for a complete recovery.

By the grace of God, giving Mama wisdom and compassion as she intervened, we rejoiced to see glimmers of response begin to occur—like a beautiful butterfly awakening from darkness. Mama's devotion and applied attention was like sunshine and nourishment to the little child. He began to smile and move his limbs. Soon Mama's daily ministrations to the child nurtured ever increasing results, manifesting in behaviors more age-related, including the attempts and advancement to crawl. He went from gravely deficient to ambitious activity under Mama's care.

Witnessing these profoundly impressionable dynamics as a young girl was a very troubling and moving experience. I learned a lot about caring and neglect.

There was no excuse for the trauma that this child endured. This incident exposed the total abandon of motherly conscience. At no time, had Mary endeavored to maintain an adequate home for her children. I had discerned her bold indifference, but for a season her cunning nature had played on Mama's tender heart with stories of misfortune and urgent necessities. But the travesty she provoked by such extreme neglect of her baby boy was beyond tolerable.

The little boy victim sufficiently recovered, for which Mama and I were ecstatic and grateful to God. Mama awakened to the realization that Mary was taking advantage of her. One day I came home, and Mary's trailer was conspicuously gone. As was typical in our home, I was not provided any explanation. Mama, however, had a heart for Mary's children and never gave up on them.

Ten years later, Mama again asked me to join her to visit Mary. Mama wanted to introduce me to the woman's daughter for some reason. The blonde-haired daughter was sweet and unspoiled. She had a kind spirit about her. While there, I saw the young boy that was once the baby we rescued; he appeared healthy and normal.

I don't know what happened to these children in the intervening years. I overheard portions of conversation spoken in deliberately hushed sentences by adults, suggesting that improper relationships had caused a continuum of unstable drama. I hope, by the grace of a loving God, that the children went on to experience wonderful and blessed lives. I hope that their mother accepted Jesus Christ as her savior before she passed on. "Jesus came to seek and to save all that are lost."

The Pennies

The perimeter that surrounded our yard was filled with tall, wild grasses, easily defined as weeds. This area appeared deserted, except for the frame of the skinny girl with the brown braids who appeared frozen beneath the blaze of sunshine, her head pivoting from one direction to another, as if she feared to be discovered.

Holding the rusty, dented can tightly against my chest, I crouched down and quietly glanced through the tall grasses, surveying the yard, hoping to be invisible to the prying eyes of sibilngs. Listening intently, I examined the premises from one perimeter to another, strategizing about where to place the rusty can I clung.

Nearby stood a lone tree, confident and strong. Its textured bark revealed an intricate pattern and its shade cast abstract shadowy images across the tall grasses. God, in His magnificent wisdom, designed the tree and the shade to provide respite to all people—rich or poor. Squinting my eyes, I examined the outstretched limbs hastily, peering intently into the shadowy foliage, determined to detect the presence of any sibling that might be poised amongst the branches. Suddenly there was a noisy clamor of chattering and the fluttering skirmish that rattled the dusty, green leaves of the tree.

The movement proved to be a squabble among some quarrelsome birds disputing the occupancy of a nest. Two antagonistic birds were attempting to frighten away the birds attending the nest, but to no avail—the nesting birds refused to be banished. The mauraders abandoned their malicious intent, flying from the dark recess of intertwined branches and leaves. One of the nesting birds remained on the disputed nest, while its mate darted after the hostile birds in an aggressive manner to warn the intruders to never return. The mate then returned gracefully, satisfied it had established the boundaries to discourage future interference. Intermittent musical chirping emanated from the leaf-veiled, discreet position of the stoutly built nest.

Peace restored, activity in the tree ceased. From my vantage point, examining the tree and surveying the whole of the yard, there was no sign of my siblings, nor anyone else. Slowly, cautiously I crept forward, prepared to escape quickly and covertly concealing my little tin can if anyone appeared.

Inside the rusty tin can was a collection of copper coins, fastidiously and slowly accrued from returning glass soda bottles to the store, which paid a penny per bottle. Collecting bottles was a challenge but I excitedly pounced on one whenever I found one, hiding it in my stash with others until I had a few bottles to exchange for a few more cents. Inside the store, I resisted the temptation of surrendering even one of my coins for a morsel of candy. The storekeeper was adept at enticing customers to buy a myriad of sweets; rows of brightly adorned, ornamentally wrapped candies were arrayed in cases like I DON"T know waht is going ong, but let's take a look.

resplendent and precious jewels. However, I remained resolute, eager to increase my supply of coins.

Remaining totally unobserved was key to successfully completing my mission in the shade of the stout tree. Determining it was safe to continue with my clandestine efforts, I hastened to the destination that I had previously decided on. Protecting my revenue was a precarious job, with my clever siblings constantly around, so I surmised that hiding my treasure in the ground was the most secure option available. Quickly, I dug a hole, buried the tin can in the ground and covered it with dirt and grass in a manner that no one would think the ground had been disturbed. My life savings were safe.

My efforts completed, I was further motivated to remain on the path to financial freedom! After all, I was only eight years old so I could acquire a fortune of wealth by the time I was eleven. I would leave the can untouched until I could make an addition to it! Fearing the propensity of some of my siblings, my savings hoard must remain my, and only my, secret. I had to maintain a constant discretion. I did not factor into my equation the variables of pride, persuasion, illusions of grandeur, or the subversive tactics of older siblings!

And so, I popped my own balloon. My pursuit of wealth with its triumphant beginning and impending blaze of glory was too exciting to remain constrained inside my eight-year-old mind. Unable to contain my sense of accomplishment, in a weak moment I revealed my mission!

Later that day, while sitting next to my older sister and brother—Lucy and Kevin—I casually mentioned my ealier activity and dreams of fortune. I may as well have climbed on the roof and announced the matter to the entire world!

Immediately, Lucy drew herself up, cocked her head toward me, and stared at me in disbelief. She studied my face, a strange light in her eyes, her voice was unusually pleasant as she questioned me further. Her pale cheeks flushed a hue of bronze, her expression was composed, she appeared very calm. I was flush with excitement to feel her interest in me.

For the first time in my life, my blonde-haired sister showed an interest in me, and she wasn't showing an element of spite! Her uncommon warmth encouraged me to confide my whole, recent, elaborate enterprise. Under the influence of her magnanimous and welcoming gesture of sisterly collaboration, I "spilled the beans."

Lucy's vague sea-blue eyes changed to a glittering emerald-green, glowing like the rarified mists of swamp fires. Her eyes intent as lashes fluttered, she inquired "so, you have this money? Where did you put it?" The tenor of her voice was soft, sweet as November persimmons, with only a tinge of tartness.

She leaned forward with a sigh, her eyelids flickering. Suddenly I felt unsure, uncertain of my resolution to keep my venture a secret. My silence prompted an ever-increasing ambience of felicity as if we were sharing a piece of warm berry cobbler—but, unbelievably, we were engaged in sisterly warmth!

With a dreamy countenance on her lovely, smooth, face, she calmly began to illustrate an imaginary world of an endless supply and variety of delicious concoctions—chocolate, cherry, peanuts and crackerjacks, suckers and lollipops of all flavors, bubble gum with bubbles blown from the gum. Every description of goodies was enhanced by her elaborate and exaggerated depiction and my imagination fueled by the pleasure of being confidants.

My brother, Kevin, overhearing our conversation, augmented her performance of endearment. It was wonderful to feel their earnest and sincere camaraderie! My heart blossomed under this fresh anointing of love, to be embraced in their affection! My resolve to protect my financial fortress crumbled, brick by brick, as visions of candy and illusions of sibling loyalty flourished in my heart. Soon, I happily led my sister and brother to my cache, unearthing my treasure!

The distance to the store evaporated beneath our fleet feet as we glided to the candy store to celebrate our new-found friendship! The negotiations continued at the glass counter where we discussed the many displays of delightful, sweet delicacies shining in their colorful packages. The pennies were clasped tightly in my fists, so I was still appreciated, important, dearly beloved, and we were compatriots.

As each of us decided on our selections from the vast array of sweets, I carefully counted out my pennies, depositing each one on the counter, mentally figuring the costs and hoping to cover the amount of money required. I felt so proud to be able to share this gift with my brother and sister.

The friendly clerk examined the group of pennies, then dropped each item into a small brown paper bag and closed it and handed it to me with a friendly gesture. He had a kind, knowing look in his eyes. Before my siblings and I got to the door, they were picking out the candies they had each selected, and it was a little confusing as they chose their prettily wrapped items out of the bag that I was clutching, trying to hold it steady as they grappled with the goodies inside.

The bell on the door of the candy store rang merrily as we left. Outside, each person had grabbed the pieces they wanted. We all quickly unwrapped the pieces most personally desirable and thrust the delicacies hungrily into our mouths. The candies spontaneously burst into delightful flavors as we chewed them. Reveling in this savory moment, I turned toward my sister and brother, wanting to exchange more of our shining, enlarged fellowship as we walked home.

My brother was already a distance away, heading wherever he had decided to go. My loving sister was walking in a different direction, totally disregarding me. I stopped, calling out to them. I don't remember if they responded. Heartbroken, I stood there, watching them go.

Realizing they had shrewdly, with smooth and slippery appeal to my emotions, strategically and fraudulently defeated my resolve for their own momentary delight. How terribly I had been deceived. Dejectedly I crossed the street and walked home, alone. The sweet visions of my illusions had deflated, then disappeared along with the flavor of the candy. My mouth was dry, and my joy diluted.

I felt dreary, diminished, and insignificant. As they ran away, both in different directions, their excuses weakening on the breeze, self-loathing overwhelmed me. How could I have been so gullible? The musical harmony had become discordant. They had only condescended to me to get the candy.

Now they were gone, abruptly, in only a brief departure of time, revealing how transient our radiant relationship had been. I felt shipwrecked. Regret and then contempt and disgrace for my susceptibility and ignorance—for allowing myself to be motivated emotionally to reject my own plan to save my money. I had been so malleable, it disgusted me.

But, considering the few copper pennies, in the long term, I didn't really pay that much for a very powerful lesson. I should have trusted the instincts that had warned me that I needed to hide the pennies if I planned to save them.

Whatever Mama's reasonings were, one can only surmise, but whatever the factors, it was not a dynamic that promoted inclusiveness, and somehow invalidated and separated our mutual connections as a family of close people.

Mama's behavior and her complexity of character persisted and was incontrovertibly established. This immutable attitude was never altered, continued her whole life, and always with lingering consequences that subtly splintered the affections of sibling to sibling. The closest I got to understand her great depth of need to be the sole authority, though she was a compassionate person, must have risen from an ancient psychological conflict issuing from the tragic loss of her family when she was a child. Beyond that superficial discussion, we have not arrived at any fine points of that theory. We just love her and always have.

How could so many children, so clumped together physically, be so distant and isolated in their hearts and minds?

Family relations, especially in a family with twelve children, are complex. Patterns of quality or inequality, coherent values—or not—begin to form in each child and between siblings. The lack of allowing or encouraging affectionate unity was unfortunately a reality in my family. In our formative years there was a void of coherence between siblings, which was exacerbated by the difficulties of the time and challenges our parents faced.

We were so many people—without personal connections! We each functioned independently, learning to disregard and contend with other people's views and subjective opinions. The lack of cohesiveness was elemental in the frequent antagonistic conflicts. It became contentious to offer a suggestion or advice, no matter how pragmatic. These predilections did not mellow as we siblings matured. The emotional distance between us created an apprehension and hostile sensitivity that limited any approach to interaction that could have proven exponentially invaluable—for all concerned—but also for future generations! The environment of our home, the constant hostilities of Mama and Daddy, the lack of his male influence, Mama's zealousness, societies' harshness, the church with its spiritual teachings—correct and incorrect; all these facets were complicit in the development of our character.

Fight Like a Girl

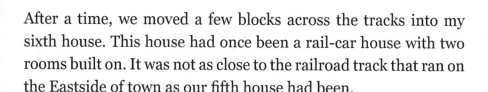

After a time, we moved a few blocks across the tracks into my sixth house. This house had once been a rail-car house with two rooms built on. It was not as close to the railroad track that ran on the Eastside of town as our fifth house had been.

There were a few other houses around, with more to come. The road was dirt and gravel and most of the houses were neat and well-attended. People tried to do the best they could.

One of the attached rooms was convenient for the boys, the other was comfortable for us girls. We were all used to sharing and didn't even think about having a personal space.

In all our old homes, Mama was very particular about maintaining clean and orderly rooms—an astonishing feat without money for impressive, expensive items and furniture, and constantly preventing a parcel of energetic children from disheveling everything in the house. Mama and Daddy usually had a nicely made-up bed in the living room which Mama decorated to present a tidy and attractive, even regal, display in our homes to dramatize that our poverty did not define who we were. We children were not allowed to sit on the bed so it wouldn't be mussed up in the event we had company. That neat, clean, adorned bed spoke loudly about Mama's self-respect and belief in self-worth. Mama taught us what Jesus taught: that no one was better than anyone else, regardless of their status in society, position, or possessions. She never relented or wavered with this belief.

This house had electricity, and it was the first time we had a television, but none of us children were interested in watching the boring black-and-white shows. We had grown up on a diet of physical interaction with nature, sunshine and breezes, swimming, fishing, shooting toy guns and fake arrows and the television programs seemed silly to us. A continuum of excitement was much more appealing than sitting motionless and watching a black screen with white flakes zigzagging through the entire picture and distorted voices conveying drama.

We children were not allowed to run around and go into other people's houses without permission, and we adhered to that rule. We kept busy playing, going to school, and doing whatever homework was required. My sister, Rachel, was just over a year older than I was; often we walked home from school together. One day, two of the neighbor boys—who lived in the house adjacent to our yard—decided to torment me and Rachel as we walked home from school. They began to yell at us and harass us even though we were merely walking down the sidewalk, talking to each other, and behaving properly as we had been taught. We had been taught from the scriptures to be humble, love mercy and do justice.

The boys were on the sidewalk across the street, and became more aggressive when we ignored them. We increased our pace, which must have encouraged their aggressive behavior. They began to throw rocks at us and called us disgusting names. The rocks they were throwing were bigger and bigger. Rachel and I were frightened and confused as to why these boys were so intent on hurting us. We were fearful we would be seriously injured by these bullies. We began to run while dodging the rocks raining down around us. They began running after us, their ambushes became increasingly aggressive.

Fearful that their furious barrage would severely injure us, we attempted to pacify them by calling out with calming sentences, but our efforts were to no avail. They were determined to injure us. We ran faster, hoping to increase the distance between us and them, but the pair of menacing boys ran faster also. Chasing after us, still pitching rocks, yelling and cursing. The rocks whizzed by us; some hit us with painful strikes before crashing on the sidewalk. No one was near to intervene, and the boys intensified their assault. Rachel and I had no idea why these boys were attacking us.

Rachel and I recognized our only option was to attempt to protect ourselves and out-running our attackers was not working. PROTECT OURSELVES! That was the only hope we had. These boys were husky and as tall or taller than we were, and we were several blocks from home.

Rachel stopped running and looked at me, a sound of resolve dominating her next words, she was resorting to the call of centuries—the call of the wild—the 'justice' that the scriptures allow us. We knew what had to be done—and we had to do it. It was the only protection that we had. We had to attempt it. Our voices echoed in unison, solemnly resolved in joint resolution.

"LET'S GET 'EM."

Our decision was immutable and our reaction was immediate. Dropping our schoolbooks, we moved as one, instantaneously, with not one ounce of hesitation. Rather than running away, we ran straight to the bullies. Shocked, they didn't have time to figure out what was happening.

Before they had time to react, Rachel and I were throwing punches, grabbing shirts, fists flying. They couldn't recounter before our tattered shoes were kicking their shins with all the blows we could muster. We didn't think, we just pounded the two stunned, violent devils until they were floundering on their backs, shirts in disarray, their soft, pink flesh looked like plump, frantic fish as they tried to wiggle away.

God allows justice, but also mercy as well. We girls struck them only with enough force to convince them that we were going home without any more arguments or deterrents from them.

Satisfied we could journey home safely, we collected our book and hurried on, leaving the bullies to pull themselves together and figure out what in the world had happened.

How wonderful and thankful I felt when Rachel and I reached our home. Mama was mopping the floor when we entered the house, disheveled, walking on the newspaper that she had spread over the floor to help keep it clean and dry. With so many children, even with Mama's constant efforts, the poor woman was working all the time. We children had some chores, but few compared to the amount of work that Mama did all the time.

I was so glad to be home. I was shaking, sighing deeply, but neither Rachel or I told Mama of our experience with the two persistent bullies. She wanted us to go to school and make good lives for ourselves, and she expected us children to protect ourselves. We always had to make an effort just to survive.

Soon, a loud banging on our screen door drew my attention. Mama looked over my shoulder toward the screen door. There stood a wild-looking, angry woman. Her eyes red-as-fire, she began shouting loud curses, demanding Mama come meet her. My young heart was trembling when she began to scream about us girls beating up her boys!

All my resolve left, like sap from a winter tree, and I felt faint. I was concerned that I was in real trouble. Mama and Daddy had always taught us children to be respectful of our elders, and not to argue with them. Would Mama understand the circumstances that had occurred and believe me about the dilemma that Rachel and I had just experienced where we had to protect ourselves? Or would she believe this screaming woman who was livid about Rachel and me beating up her boys?

The woman described me and Rachel in unfair terms, towering in the doorway, confronting Mama and us with such loud and unkind hostility. The woman claimed that we girls had initiated the fight and forced her darling boys, who were bigger than us, to try to protect themselves.

As the livid neighbor with her bulging veins, screamed about us, would Mama believe my explanation as I timidly and nervously argued the issue with the adult? I felt overwhelmed as the woman persisted that our behavior deserved substantial punishment. Rachel and I were passive by nature and tended to be caring; neither of us were prone to violence. We usually avoided any form of aggression toward us, and Mama had taught us to always make efforts to ignore insults and resist difficulties.

She had raised us with patience and wisdom and had always instructed us to rise above personal ordeals as much as possible, without getting killed.

The neighbor woman was beyond agitated; she was fierce and fuming. I stood nervously between Mama and her, frightened as the she continued her rant and accusations. Mama stood quietly, gripping the wet mop handle, listening to the stream of vitrol from the enraged woman. The woman threw her arms around as she sputtered, with various gestures intended to emphasize her rage.

Mama listened patiently, displaying respect to the woman without patronizing her. Somehow, Mama's demeanor began to calm the woman; her anger began strangely to dissipate under Mama's finesse. Mama never stated agree-meent with the stream of accusations, yet the woman seemed pacified, in addition to bewildered. The woman left quietly, without any show of hostility. I was amazed at how Mama managed to soothe the impact of the situation without implying agreement with the woman.

She was so mad I was Scared mama might believe her!

106

Mama lifted the mop and began to run it over the old lino-
leum, not saying a word, as if nothing had just happened. As if
the world had just settled back on its axis. She left me with my
pride and self-esteem. And gratitude. She was amazing. I learned
a great deal that day, being an active participant in the whole sce-
nario. Thank God for the most wonderful and wise mother.

It amazed me that so many neighbors had such dysfunctional
lifestyles, yet for whatever reason, they considered themselves
superior to my family. Mama and Daddy were decent and moral,
and held us to a high standard. They encouraged their children to
do well and be decent and moral also.

My siblings made good friends with people from various
parts of town. Mama didn't allow us children to run around the
neighborhood and visit other homes without her permission and
required that the mother, or a trusted parent, was at their home.
We children were happy playing outdoors in the breeze and the
sun—enjoying nature. Kevin found a dark, green swamp and we
swam in the murky place. Now, I think about the snakes and who
knows what. Then, I remember hanging onto a thick tree trunk
while I played in the cool water.

At school, I was in a class with my old friend, Billy, from
Walnut Street. He had a terrible time trying to do his schoolwork,
so I helped him as much as I could. The teacher knew and didn't
say anything. Billy was a nice boy and his mom and dad had been
good neighbors.

Soon, one day our car was loaded again, with all we children that now numbered eleven, and one 'in the oven,' as they
say. Whatever we could pack into the car was included, and our
family was headed for Idaho. Daddy and Mama must have had

stars in their eyes again—surely this time we would find the end
of the rainbow.

For My Sister

It seems but only yesterday
We played so many things
House and dolls and jumping rope
Sometimes sharing dreams.

Walnut stain the ringworm healed
Walking to the farm?
How we backed each other up
When e'er we faced some harm?

Remember all our valiant deeds
Adventurous act of daring?
Halloweens of trick and treat
The "boo's" and "eeks" of scaring?

Remember "jacks" and "chip'n dale"
And marbles on our knees
Remember damming up the creek
And hanging from the trees?

Remember gravy, potatoes, rolls
Pungent Navy beans?
The candy bars with worms inside,
dandelion greens?

Canned milk for cocoa,
the bucket of iced tea?
The wagon we pulled to Uncle and Aunt
where we each got a treat?

Dressing chickens,
wet feathers so scummy!
But fried crisp by Mama,
so good to the tummy?

Remember at Christmas,
so hard to go to bed
The dolls we found on Christmas morn,
with curls of brown and red

Moist chunks of delight,
envision brown fudge?
Ice-cream from snow mounds,
Mama made in the tub?

Poignant thoughts of yesterday
What of thee do I yearn?
Blithe land of youth's enchantment
To you would I return?

We rocked our dolls
and dreamed our dreams
But life's not always
what it seems.

Our hearts were bright
like morning sun
But dark clouds gathered
with the dawn.

Or, Rachel,
it just can't be true
That you have flown—
that you are gone.

Chasing Rainbows

We were going to Idaho this time and I was leaving the fourth grade.

Mama was very fond of photography, and she placed her treasured photos in an old, dome-topped trunk, and entrusted it to the care of the neighbor across the road, who happened to be Mary—the very woman who had lived in the trailer house in our yard and neglected her son. How could Mama still trust her?

Daddy had a friend who encouraged him to come to Idaho, convincing him there was more opportunity there. We children were hopeful and dreamed we would have a nice house and

Daddy would find a decent job that would be consistent and beneficial. We would have a kitchen with tasty food in the cabinets and Mama would not have to worry so much about meals and clothes. Maybe we would even have good shoes that fit and such nonsense as that!

Traveling for our family was not without its challenges—even hazards. Especially in an old car and little money. Gas had to be paid for, and our finances were thin and had to be stretched to hopefully cover whatever we experienced.

It was a long and arduous journey from Kansas to Idaho in those days when roads were narrow and curved up and down and around the steep mountain heights. Most of the sparse traffic was big diesel trucks hauling products across the country. Some terrains were more difficult and frightening than others. Old, used tires with little tread could blow out, the radiator and coolants might leak, the engine could start smoking, and a million other problems could arise—and did. Daddy did most of the mechanical work, but sometimes it caused our schedules to be compromised. Often our directions were uncertain, and we had to re-route.

The old, two-seated car carried the thirteen of us past the flat fields of Kansas, where bales of hay were scattered about, waiting to be picked up and stored in farmer's barns to keep them dry through the summer. If they were rained on, before they were removed and placed under sheltering roofs, they could mold and lose some of their vitamin value when winter came, and they were fed to the hungry cattle and horses.

I was unaware that during those summers, the man I would marry, at a distance away, was lifting and carrying heavy hay bales to throw upon wagons to be taken and unloaded into barns. It was such a hot and heavy job, and paid so little, that fewer and fewer people would take the jobs for the farmers. Eventually equipment was manufactured that would do the job with large machines.

The greenish hay, blowing in the wind in the fields, turned orangish, then the farmers came to cut the hay and wire it into hay bales. The new balers that are used now, although expensive of course, took a great deal of the manual labor out of the process.

Daddy didn't seem to be hindered by adventure or crusades to find a better life. He drove over the steep tops of mountains and swinging bridges made of rope. Unfortunately, none of these proclivities qualified to meet the financial needs of a family.

Regrettably, he didn't seem to have the same propensity or opportunity for jobs. Being unable to read or write didn't work to his advantage, although it wasn't that uncommon in those days when some people didn't even think it was important for children to go to school for an "education."

Sometimes, as we traveled into the unknown, the landscape seemed to stretch forever, sometimes hot and barren, sometimes as if we were barely hanging onto the gravely, narrow road high upon the side of a mountain, shivering in the cold mountain air where we saw snow and snow-peaked mountain tops and mist covered mountain valleys that seemed to have no bottom, hidden by enormous trees.

Gas stations were few and far between, and those we encountered were greasy and dirty. The window openings had tin plastered over them, signage was chipped and rusted, and inside the crevices were crowded with trinkets and junk. Even in our poverty, Mama always worked hard to keep things clean and organized, which made places like these unkempt gas stations uninviting. But we had to get gas.

As we progressed on our journey into the unknown, no matter how intense the ordeal for her, Mama was stoic as we continued our search for the end of the rainbow. Though she was pregnant, she never complained about discomfort and did not express doubts or fears about what might lie ahead. Mama's courage made us children feel safe. On we forged, uncertain, but hoping for a bright prospect from this venture.

Driving past the scattered, small towns, wondering what the future would bring this time, soon the miles of road melted into the darkness of night, with only the dim, murky, bug-swirling, wispy light of the car's head lamp's glow shining through the black emptiness. Each of us children, in quiet solitude, rested our heads wherever there was a bare space, and limply folded and conformed into any available space and agreeable configuration.

If a sibling objected to your nearness or weight with truculence or hostility, you merely reconfigured the presence of your limbs into a more acceptable and less intrusive composition. You stared into the night wondering about your designation, gazing searchingly for anything of interest revealed in the distance, then drifted into a dreamy slumber, trusting that this time, going so far, Mama and Daddy would know what they were doing. How could so many children, so clumped together physically, sometimes wrapped in warm blankets, be so isolated in their minds and hearts and dreams?

But Mama and Daddy were there, so I had nothing to fear. In Idaho, I would be away from the next-door bullies. Surely, life would be better.

Along the way we would pull over to enjoy the glorious nature surrounding us. We waded in blue, clear lakes. We climbed over smooth, volcanic rock that gave no indication how many years it had been since it was thrown out over the land. We slept on our blankets wherever we needed to stop and rest. And we saw the most beautiful mountain ranges, with their bluish-purple mists covering white pinnacles of snow.

We felt like we were not poor—we were rich in the glories of nature. We got to experience more than holey shoes. How did old shoes matter when compared to the fresh air, beauty, and grandeurs we were allowed to experience?

Sometimes, the landscape on the journey to Idaho seemed to stretch forever. It was hot and barren sometimes, but sometimes the mountain scenery was breath-taking. Gas stations were small and far-between, greasy and dirty and still wanted your money.

On our way to Idaho, our dream land, we forged onward. By now there were eleven of us children. We were unsure of what was ahead but remained hopeful, trusting in Mama and Daddy and God. Hoping for a bright prospect from this venture. Our minds were expanded by the sights we saw. Corn fields with giant green stalks reaching towards the sun. Wheat fields that met the horizon, the golden grain moving in massive waves in the wind. There were unexpected views of wild animals, commanding rivers with white rapids, and white snow peaking the variegated mountain ranges.

Mama was quiet, never confiding any fears or doubts as again we traveled on to find the end of the rainbow—driving over the tops of mountains, on swinging bridges, and down gravel roads. There were unexpected halts as the old car broke down, which Daddy somehow managed to fix and on we went. Perhaps Daddy's pursuits for finding a better life taught us something better than money could buy.

Treasures in Trash

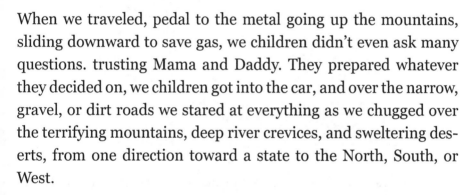

When we traveled, pedal to the metal going up the mountains, sliding downward to save gas, we children didn't even ask many questions. trusting Mama and Daddy. They prepared whatever they decided on, we children got into the car, and over the narrow, gravel, or dirt roads we stared at everything as we chugged over the terrifying mountains, deep river crevices, and sweltering deserts, from one direction toward a state to the North, South, or West.

It was exciting to run barefoot over the ancient formations of hardened, smooth swells of volcanic rock from some previous eruption. Wading in remote resplendently cool, clear, fresh lakes that invited us along the way. The interaction with nature we experienced first-hand made the stories in our schoolbooks come to life when our studies included these geographies.

We were deficient in finances, but in our many amblings, we were rich in observation, and the authenticity of the amazing creations of God. As we witnessed natural environment, we developed an appreciation of self-motivation and self-preservation.

Our diverse travels introduced us to a surplus of lifestyles and mentalities present in other people. As we encountered the vast array of human behaviors—including indifference, hostility, suspicion, and predatory—we learned to comprehend the intricate and diverse spectrum of the character of people.

We also looked for city dumps to scour. We would scale the mounds of trash, carefully shuffling through the refuse to discover half-buried objects that had potential.

Things tossed away as insignificant by others became for us treasures retrieved, revived, and appreciated. Sometimes musty and damp, these gems sparked much entertainment and joy in our lives. Our hearts were stirred and soared with gratitude as our salvage from other people's rubbish gave us many hours of exciting endeavors.

We shoveled out many daydreams mingled in the silent dust of those dumps. Our minds were nourished as we envisioned rustic, broken frames that could be straightened; twisted and tangled parts that could be repaired; and faintly faded objects that could still serve a purpose. Tattered, battered, scratched, twisted, neglected—it didn't matter. The cuts, scratches, bruises, and momentary stinging pain we incurred when pulling our gems forcefully from the ground were trivial considering the rapturous magnitude of the prizes we clutched so tightly in our sagging arms.

We celebrated exceptional discoveries and would eventually stagger and stumble as we carried our prodigious gifts to the car. This grim, but bountiful, mission brought us children endless excitement and enjoyment. Digging through other people's cast-off trash was like crusts of bread to our hungry souls.

Perhaps, not comprehended by us in those moments, our efforts reflected our nurturing of hope that we, cast off by society, could be something more than anyone else envisioned.

A Brief Exchange

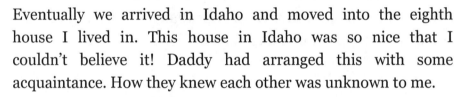

Eventually we arrived in Idaho and moved into the eighth house I lived in. This house in Idaho was so nice that I couldn't believe it! Daddy had arranged this with some acquaintance. How they knew each other was unknown to me.

The youngest sibling of our family, Denise, was born soon after we while we moved into this beautiful home. Idaho law required pregnant women to have their babies in a hospital. Denise was the only baby Mama birthed in a hospital. Fortunately, both returned healthy.

My oldest brother, Randall, soon found a job; he was always willing to work. One day Daddy and Randall had a stormy fight over Randall's paycheck—Daddy wanted the money Randall earned and Randall refused to give it to him. Randall left and hitch-hiked back to Kansas. I was broken-hearted to see Randall so angry and to see him leave. I didn't know if I would ever see him again.

One day Mama informed us, shockingly, that she had hired out Rachel and me to a strange family in exchange for a washing machine. I was ten years of age and Rachel was eleven. We were to live with this family for a period as part of the trade to perform their housework and such.

That trade didn't last long. As Rachel and I washed and dried the dinner dishes the first night, the man kept staring at my beautiful sister in the most perverse way. I was so frightened and upset. That night, in a strange home with a pervert, I began crying out of concern for my sister. I cried so hard and so loud and could not be comforted. Later that night, my distress unrelenting, the couple put Rachel and me in their car and off we drove. We drove over the narrow, low, earthen dam, with the moon reflecting on the dark and endless body of water. I was terrified. Thank God, they took us home. I was so relieved and thrilled to go into our house and get into my bed.

I didn't know what to tell Mama. She looked at me strangely but didn't say much. Rachel didn't say anything—she seldom said anything. She, like me, usually just did as we were told. That strange family had a daughter that was about the same age as Rachel and me. Why couldn't she do what we were supposed to do? There wasn't anything wrong with her.

I have often wondered why Mama was not more verbal and explanatory to us children. If she had been more open and shared information with us, it would have better prepared us. In situations such as this, we were never informed of reasons or contexts, leaving us children with only assumptions and interpretations to navigate the complex world.

Unfortunately, our time in this nice house was short-lived. An unknown dilemma occurred, and we were once again moving.

Daddy found an underground house where we could live in the same town; that was my ninth house. It had a dirt yard, and the roof was flat, tarred black, but dry—at least as I remember. Sometimes when it was too hot to sleep at night, we children slept on top of the flat roof, sometimes sharing thoughts as we gazed into the glowing stars that smiled upon us in the darkness.

Across the street from our house lived a nice woman with a young son. She made and painted ceramic objects for additional income.

I COULD NOT STOP CRYING – I WANTED TO GO HOME.

We children found there were huge earthworms that came to the surface and then crawled over the ground at night. That's why they were called "night-crawlers." We would go to the park, especially after a rain, and collect dozens of these enormous worms. Then we would proceed to go fishing, constructing our fishing poles from branches and any fishing line we find. Fish was always a welcome addition to our table.

We discovered that the nearby railroad tracks were frequently used by trains to transport potatoes and coal to other parts of the country. By God's help, we children were allowed to collect potatoes that had fallen on the ground, and the lost chunks of coal. In the evenings, we would take burlap bags to where the train cars waited. We darted around and beneath the cars, gathering potatoes and coal. We were cautious, in case one of the cars began to pull away. We then heaved our treasures home—potatoes for meals and coal for heating.

One day I discovered a small, bleeding bird. It had been shot, and I gently picked it up and carried it home. Mama told me to put flour on its bloody wounds, so I did. I kept the little guy in the little shack near our house, and he began to heal. One day I cradled him in my hands and walked out of the shack, where I reluctantly opened my hands to release him back into the sky. Away he flew.

The Dilemma

One day, there was a knock at the door of our basement house. Mama answered the door and welcomed in a group of nicely dressed women. The women entered and introduced themselves. They seemed a little aloof, furtively looking about the rooms. Mama always did the best house cleaning she could, beside cooking our potatoes and hand-sewing clothes for us.

Mama was wearing her old, full, drab dress, pinned at the bosom to hold the dress modestly closed. Mama always wore extra safety pins because pins were commonly used for all types of repairs. I don't remember if she had her old, shapeless slippers on, or was barefoot which was common. Some of us children stood quietly and politely yet listening to what was being said.

The women informed Mama that if we would join their "church," their church would take care of every need we had! Clothes, shoes, food, lunches, and a lengthy list of financial help would follow—if we joined their "church."

They sounded so persuasive! My mind couldn't comprehend what they were offering. It was quite confusing. I noticed their frequent glances across the room, and of us.

Our room—our house—was shabby, but neat. Our furniture was always cast-offs, chipped, and nailed back together. The faded, frayed couch sank in the middle and sat crooked even though Mama placed small boards under the feet to make it even. Mama could hammer and sew and instinctively knew where to place everything to create a pleasant ambiance of home.

The women, attempting to be discreet, were evaluating us and our surroundings, no doubt finding us lacking in value. My eyes and ears were glued on Mama as she stood there in her shapeless, faded dress, being critically appraised by the staunch group of women. Mama's thick, brown hair was pinned neatly upon her head in a bun, her pale face down, her appearance humble and vulnerable. She was so diligent to present herself decently and fashionably, regardless of her threadbare clothing and limited wardrobe. No matter her attire, she made it elegant, and she held herself like a queen.

This offer by the well-dressed women, being presented to Mama, was remarkable to us children. Clothes, shoes, food, money—how could that be possible? The women assured her their proposition was valid and we could lack for nothing. Provided we join their "church."

Without knowing what she would cook for supper, and with a perennial history of scarcity, I could see that Mama was thinking with deep contemplation. The women waited, already expecting her grateful compliance.

Mama's voice was quiet, but her voice rang in my heart. "We are Pentecostal." Mama spoke appreciatively and considerately, but, lifting her head, with a genuine determination.

Those were not the words the women expected to hear, but Mama couldn't be convinced to change her mind. The women were polite, but obviously disappointed at failing to achieve their agenda. The word "Pentecostal" affected them somehow. Mama was saying that we were Christians, that we believed in in God, and His Holy Son, Jesus Christ, whose love, and sacrifice extends salvation to all. I don't know what "Pentecostal" meant to them, but they wasted no time departing. Their religious doctrine obviously didn't cover charity without strings.

I thank God always for Mama's decision. Jesus said to help the poor and feed the hungry. Not to coerce, but out of love. The fact that Mama didn't join their religion didn't change what Jesus told us all to do. It was unfortunate that "religious" people did not find it necessary to obey the words of Jesus and offer us any help at all, regardless.

Bread, Butter, and Bullies

Going to a new grade school in a community whose religion is institutionalized and differs from your own, is a challenge. At school I encountered a very hostile, tough, girl who was such a bully, that even the boys in our fifth-grade class acquiesced to her aggression, afraid not to follow her directions. They were her "entourage."

When our class was recessed for some time to exercise our energies on the playground, she created opportunity to torture me. "Holy Roller!" She ran about, screaming at me. I tried to ignore her constant taunts and threats, and those of her entourage. One day at lunchtime, a nice, quiet friend of mine was sitting beside me at the table. The bully filled her spoon with ketchup and mustard and flipped it toward my friend. The goopy mixture hit me and my friend, who was wearing a new white blouse.

I can't explain how or why I moved so fast! Suddenly, I was standing at the side of the "bully," rubbing a slice of bread and butter over her face. The table of lunch eaters were hushed with shock—but no more than I and the bully, who was in such shock she did nothing.

I had been trying to win the prize that week for the person with the best behavior! I was deflated with what I had done, knowing that now, because of it, I would not receive my name at the top of the teacher's blackboard.

The next day, as the students entered the classroom, each one looked for their name's position in the best-behaved list on the chalkboard, where the top name was the week's winner for best behavior. Feeling dismayed about the prior day's bread-and-butter incident, I reluctantly looked at the bottom for my name before glancing at the top name on the list. At first in disbelief—then beyond ecstatic—I saw MY NAME at the top of the list of well-behaved students! The teacher was aware of what had occurred at lunch time the day before. OH! What a kind woman!

One day, after weeks of enduring the abuse of the bully, I waited after school, watching for her. My intent was simply to walk home with her. She was surprisingly of milder temperament since her entourage wasn't present. As we walked toward her home, casually, and with a friendly demeanor, I engaged her in conversation and was able to learn more about her. Before arriving at her small, neat, cottage—which belonged to her grandparents—her emotions surfaced, and I realized her anger and hostility came from a deep cavern of sadness in her heart. She was emotionally distraught, feeling abandoned by her parents, even though she loved her grandparents. Her parents had left her, and she had interpreted what she considered their lack of caring with not being wanted. That emotion had been twisted into tumultuous anger, bursting with hostility.

I felt deep empathy for her, and by the grace of God, she did not attack me anymore. I was no longer the target of her grief.

And she behaved better after that afternoon. I think she recognized my genuine sympathy and understanding for her.

Spuds and Suds

The potatoes and coal that we children had been carrying home from the wasted, free refuge from the near-by railroad cars, had been a real blessing for our family for food and heat. However, I was not prepared for the day the teacher dismissed any children from our class who needed to go and help with the potato harvest that was in season.

I was more surprised to find that Mama and Daddy had signed myself and some of my brothers and sisters to work in the potato fields. They drove us to a huge field with a factory nearby that made dried potatoes from the potatoes harvested from the fields.

I asked Rachel what we were going to do, but she just shrugged as she didn't know either. She never said much about anything, she didn't question much, and didn't seem to esteem herself enough to get concerned about anything. She was so beautiful, creative, and smart, but an easy target for unethical people because she was so tender-hearted.

Daddy left us, and went into a building, then came back with a red-haired, burly, hairy, crooked-legged man who was carrying a bundle of dusty, burlap bags. We could see dad and the other man, but we couldn't hear their conversation. The man then tossed down the bags, causing a swirl of dust to rise into the air, each bag being about three feet long, and looped loosely at the top with rough, thick, twine for tying the bags after each one was filled with potatoes. We were to pick up the potatoes, individually, or in clusters—our problem to figure out—then place them in the scratchy burlap bags. We were to tie the bags around our waists so we could drag the heavy weight of the bags as we filled them.

We quietly obeyed, tied the bags to our waists, and began picking up the brown-skinned, oblong, heavy, starchy vegetables. We were assigned rows that appeared to stretch into the sky. Bending, rising, filling, dragging--then bending, rising, filling, dragging—the bags grew heavier and heavier. The sacks became so heavy from the fat potatoes, and even more so from the clods of dirt adhered on the potatoes. It became incredibly was difficult to drag them along. We each heaved the bag as far as we could, untied the heavy bag, retrieved another gunny sack, tied it around the waist, and then resumed what seemed an endless and herculean effort.

The rows of the newly plowed fields looked endless as we wiped the sweat from our eyes and scratched our red, itchy, skin that had been rubbed and indented by the coarse bags. We sighed to see the long, dark rows with all the multitude of the various-shaped and sized potatoes lying hap-hazardly along the sides and even the centers of the dirt rows. Some potatoes were still encrusted in dirt, and you had to work them out of the ground. When the clods of dirt clung to the potatoes, even after attempting to dislodge the hard, caked dirt, into the bag the potato went—dirt attached. This made the bags even heavier to try to drag along even if I was a limber and strong ten-year-old.

I don't know how many days we worked, but even if we needed the money, Mama ended our part in the harvest. She wanted us in school.

We went back to school and tried to catch up on the lessons. The teacher met Rachel and I in the coat room and offered us some coats and some clothes. That's how kind she was. God bless her.

In school, we could not afford to buy our lunches. My sister, Rachel, and I were allowed to eat after lunch period ended, provided we worked in the kitchen during the lunch period. With our hair wrapped in hairnets, we carried trays, scraped trays, and washed trays. We worked hard; whatever we were told to do, we did. The kitchen was hot with steam and soap suds floated everywhere so we had to be careful not to slide down on the floor.

We didn't mind the work and were thankful for our meals. Still, it was embarrassing that the other students would hand in their trays, and we were the only students working there. Some adults in the school administration did not think we should eat unless we worked for our meals.

Rachel never complained.

All children should be treated equally in our educational systems, having the same opportunities, regardless of their economic status. My siblings were extremely intelligent, but there were no programs to help the children who were poor. It is astounding that some billionaires who have so much are so selfish when presented with the opportunity to help those who would benefit greatly, especially children. Most children are very smart and capable. Thank God for the people and programs that help others, but more are needed.

The Christmas Doll

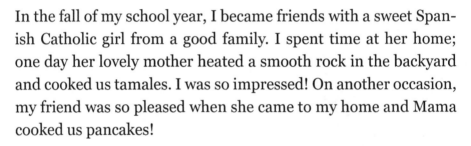

In the fall of my school year, I became friends with a sweet Spanish Catholic girl from a good family. I spent time at her home; one day her lovely mother heated a smooth rock in the backyard and cooked us tamales. I was so impressed! On another occasion, my friend was so pleased when she came to my home and Mama cooked us pancakes!

Soon, the fall season was over, and my favorite time of the year was approaching. Christmas! That wonderful time of the year when Mama and Daddy mysteriously made a tall, wide, green, Christmas tree appear. The Christmas tree would sparkle, wrapped with silvery tinsel and shiny icicles, glimmering like diamonds. It was always placed in a special and exact position that made our home like a fairy land and brought us children excitement and thrills. I loved Christmas—not only did it represent the birth of the Lord Jesus, but Mama and Daddy always made everything about it so special and magnificent.

One Saturday, Mama gave me permission to spend time with my friend, allowing us to walk to the nearby small town and enjoy the day. We were both ten years of age and in the fifth grade that Idaho December, and our excitement could not be contained as we walked to town for an afternoon of viewing all the holiday finery and merchandise displayed in the store windows along the town's boardwalk.

My friend and I had so much fun. We went from storefront to storefront, talking, laughing, gazing at everything shown on display in the store windows. My friend and I were not allowed to go into the stores according to rules set down by our parents, so we entertained ourselves by studying each aspect of wonderment displayed in the department store windows.

The windows were framed in silver-sheened tinsel and masses of thick, green strands of garland intertwined with miniature twinkling lights, enhancing—and exploiting—the distinctive features of the treasures for purchase—toys, perfumes, candies, jewelry, wallets—gifts for customers to purchase and bestow upon friends and family.

Without the first penny, my friend and I entertained ourselves as we examined each mesmerizing display of wonder, our eyes devouring the countless, ingenious toys and their amazing abilities! Some could walk, squeak, and even flap their wings and move in other fascinating manners—with just the pull of a string. How exciting—how fun—to view such rapturous objects. Small, life-like trains with precisely designed locomotives, chugged down miniature tracks, pulling an array of variously colored cars with windows carved in them, and a red caboose that completed the pageant. The trains traversed between green pine trees and wooden cabins, dark smoke pouring from the top pipes of the engines. We excitedly imagined how we would play with each toy or dress like a princess in the fancy clothes that were on display.

I was drawn towards the exquisitely molded dolls with their pink cheeks and red, brown, golden, or black silky hair. Each doll was dressed flatteringly and fashionably with assorted garments of wonderfully elegant materials—colorful bows and fabrics, ruffles, laces, and delicate jeweled buttons effused with sparkling crystals.

As we continued our stroll down the boardwalk, we came upon THE store. I fell in love with an entrancing, beautiful, brown-haired doll. The enticing lighting invented the impression that this doll was alive, as her sparkling, attentive eyes flickered in my gaze. She absolutely thrilled my heart.

This remarkable creation exuded every aesthetic detail. She seemed resourcefully aware, even impressionable; when lifted or held aloft, her wide, glassy, brown eyes were wide open with fascination to view the world.

As if this manifestation was insufficient to captivate and convince of their beauty, additional abilities were awe-inspiring. When the ingenious doll was laid backward to rest or sleep, it's amazing engineering and construction manipulated its inner unseen workings to diligently close the crafted eyelids, resourcefully lowering their long, generous black lashes to lie against her sweet face, simulating sleep.

I was smitten and my heart embraced this wonderful doll. She was so realistic and engaging; I knew she could be my friend in all circumstances.

The brown-haired doll, the only one I was interested in because of the simple fact that the hair was like my own brown hair, even though my hair hung in braids instead of curls, standing so quiet and patiently in the white box, stunningly arranged to reveal all her best qualities, even the appealing embossed mauve bonnet that matched and enhanced the colorful embellishing on her luxuriously glossy dress.

Resourcefully, other delightful touches were effective to convince the interested observer, such as myself. Embroidered patterns flourished on the sheer, flouncy, ruffles surrounding the whole, full skirt, with a complimentary color augmented by a lighter hue repeated on the edge of the bonnet, in ruffle form. What an ideal theme this whole configuration facilitated.

The bodice was cross-laced with thin pink ribbons and the prim, rounded collar had tiny, sculpted, distinctly constructed flowers, like raised red rosebuds with glimpses of green leaves beside each one. The ruffled pantaloons were white as wool and had fluffy ruffles on the legs.

The silky sleeves were short and fluffy, with ruffled edges. The abundance of adroit emblems and complimentary colors illuminated her pale, blushing gentle face. Delicate tissues surrounded the sheltered doll in her fresh box, further enhancing the abundant, appealing, glamorous presentation.

My riveted eyes were not only drawn to the brown-haired beauty, but powerlessly riveted in admiration of this enchanting, incredible source of girlish delight. The quaint and charming little doll enraptured me. Each moment of entrancement revealed something astonishing.

Her legs and arms could stiffly move, arms reaching out to be held and legs permitting her to sit down and herself aright. The doll's thin, flexible socks and petite white shoes with tiny ties could be removed and placed back on her delicate feet. This gorgeously attired doll seemed so life-like to me; she would be a true and lasting friend.

This doll offered an enchanting, invaluable source of delight,

The doll glowed in the store window

and the possibilities impacted me unmercifully, evoking a flood of emotion that enamored me and impressed me beyond the many other remarkable toys that also demonstrated very creative and enthusiastic qualities.

My friend and I entertained outlandish dreams of prosperity, laughing joyously over our impossible but remarkable thoughts, our minds' inventing even more ridiculous possibilities.

We imagined the responses and expressions of our siblings and parents, should we surprise our families with such choice gifts, so handsomely wrapped and placed under the Christmas tree. Two sweet little girls quite aware of the limits of poverty and financial strain, momentarily exploiting our cherished ideas. I knew that possessions did not override Godly behavior but I sure desired that pretty doll.

Our minds were alive with beautiful objects, and our continual philosophical discussions were fun combined with longing, and we continued to discuss the merits of all that had impressed us as we wended our way homeward.

With so much to see, and so deeply entranced, time rapidly disappeared. We continued our stroll, and as we approached the end of the boardwalk, some of the stores had turned off their lights and were dark inside. We realized it was later than we had expected. We weren't allowed to be out late, so we accelerated our pace, leaving the small town to venture home.

Laughing and chatting, still entranced by the wonderful things we had viewed, we continued sharing our imaginations as we started across the darkened road that had to be crossed before coming to the sidewalk that ran in front of some small houses that sat at the edge of the town.

The houses were dim, shuttered against the darkness that had crept in. A long walk remained before we would arrive at our houses, with little light along the way.

Light-heartedly exploring our subjects, we were very engaged in the pros and cons of our opinions. Almost imperceptible, a subtle, uncertain sound made us glance instinctively over our shoulders.

Perhaps the angel watching over me forewarned us with this unintentional, indiscriminate commotion, shattering the black hush of the night like a tuning fork to our ears.

The dark shadows of young men emerged behind us.

At Knife's Point

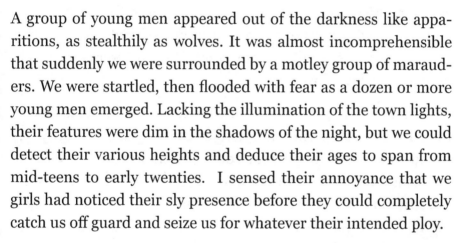

A group of young men appeared out of the darkness like apparitions, as stealthily as wolves. It was almost incomprehensible that suddenly we were surrounded by a motley group of marauders. We were startled, then flooded with fear as a dozen or more young men emerged. Lacking the illumination of the town lights, their features were dim in the shadows of the night, but we could detect their various heights and deduce their ages to span from mid-teens to early twenties. I sensed their annoyance that we girls had noticed their sly presence before they could completely catch us off guard and seize us for whatever their intended ploy.

Warnings were flashing like the bright, red glowing lights that warned a railroad train was coming rapidly down the tracks. The streets were isolated and quiet—no one was around that could hear us or see the dangerous situation—we were virtually alone. Alone except for Jesus who said He will never leave us alone or forsake us.

A tall, quiet, and well-spoken male was the leader and he presented himself calmly and with a contrived pleasantness. Beneath his guise of friendliness, I knew was formulating an alternate nefarious plan for his cohort.

This master manipulator began addressing me with a variety of comments and questions. There appeared to be nothing crude or coarse about this quietly assertive young man. The restless, rustling group was weighing my responses to his comments, and his attitude.

The terror that iced my veins like permafrost was not even subtly evident as I perfunctorily, blithely responded to his clever sallies. Mama had taught her children how to protect themselves, and I had become adept at portraying a tough-hided, fearless exterior. responses, I attempted to neutralize the intimidation and threat with my nonchalant attitude sparked a momentary challenge of wits. Point, counterpoint. He and I were engaged in psychological warfare.

In the dim light of the isolated road the tall leader appeared to control the program and his voice commanded authority. My friend and I drew closer to each other, attempting to show a calm demeanor, our eyes secretly surveying the scene, trying to assess the situation. The muscles in my friend's arm were tense, and I didn't know what she was going to do. I sensed her fear and was concerned that she might start to run; I had this strong impression that if we ran at that moment, our fear and movement would incite and stimulate the group into action. "Don't run," I whispered through my teeth, my mouth angling the words as if talking through a puppet. "Don't run."

I corralled as much nonchalance as I could muster, keeping my voice even and unconcerned. I spoke to the leader as if he and his gang were of no concern—as if I was ignorant of his foxy maliciousness. My mind was racing, discerning how to deconstruct his perspective and perhaps influence him—to establish some harmonious connection and dismantle the propensity of danger we were facing.

This shrewd-eyed commando appeared slightly disconcerted, as if not used to being challenged. In his eyes, piercing as a snake, I saw the flicker of a spark of uncertainty. The leader wavered momentarily, as if his conscience awoke. But his accomplices were becoming annoyed; rustling amongst the crew indicated there was fierce opposition to deviating from their original intention. They appeared ready to enact their scheme upon the signal from their commando leader. The leader recognized their impatience. Perhaps the fear of losing his authority caused the leader's dialogue to stumble. He attempted to reassert himself with more blatantly contentious statements.

With nonchalant conversation and an attitude of pleasantness, I continued in my attempt to defuse whatever the group was devising, to diminish their enthusiasm, and to disrupt their unity.

The agitation in their crew fractured into arguments amongst the ranks for a minute. With a short opportunity to take advantage of their momentary confusion, I nudged my friend to take a few steps away from the group while whispering "Don't run!"

However, it became apparent that the attempt to dissipate their intent was futile. At the end of the leader's left arm, there was a distinctive silver flash of light that sparked brightly against the black night, reflecting from the master manipulator's grasp. My friend and I saw the shiny flash, and silently gasped at the implications. Even though the leader had not raised the knife into the air, he did reveal it at his side. Aware that his authority was being evaluated, he knew he must reestablish his command. The other young men, observing the actions of their leader, began to move uncertainly.

I felt the blood drain from my legs, and I felt like a limp, rag doll, but the bluish glare of the knife blade poised a heightened threat that could not be ignored. I persisted in my fearless demeanor. The impatient movements in the group increased; they seemed bewildered and confounded and irritated. Their attention turned toward their commander, waiting for a signal from the tall authority to respond with alacrity. With their focus diverted from us and onto the others in their cohort, I knew we had a brief opportunity. Survival instinct washed over me with a mighty, powerful force as I tugged my friend's arm and spoke with conviction and urgency one of the most important words in the universe: "run." "Run! Run! Run!"

Thank God my friend and I were used to walking! Run, we did! Our skinny, little legs went flying. Our tough-leather feet skimmed over the ground, barely touching the gravel beneath our shoes. Faster and faster, we ran as we heard the trouncing of shoe soles thundering behind us.

The pounding of feet on the ground rumbled as the army of young men pursued us. We didn't look back for a second, lest we missed a step or slid on a rock. We ran like lightning, like old Satan himself was after us—and he was—or so his minions. We ran and ran from the dim light into the darker night, our breath was foggy white, our chests sharply panting, as sweat rolled down our temples. The distance was swallowed up by the darkness as we lengthened our strides, bounding like deer, praying that our feet would not slip or slide on the gravel. We ran and we ran—like wild things we ran! Gasping for breath, our hearts pumping with adrenaline, we ran! Terrified, we ran! "Don't fall! Don't stumble! Don't slide! Don't trip!"

Frantic to elude the devastating figures of fury, we ran! Struggling for deeper breaths, we ran! Deserted in the desolate night we ran!

Struggling to gain against the enemy, we ran! Deeper into the dim, eerie darkness, we ran! There was no earthly being to help us!

Passionately, our lips clenched, my friend's black hair blowing, flowing, and streaming straight into the air over her back, we ran!

Then, a dim, slim, slit of mellow light emerged through the darkness, its warm appearance beside the dark, dusty street, was too fantastic to be true. It was my friend's home! Home! We burst through the door into the light and her family's concerned shock!

We realized we were safe! No one was following us—and in fact, we had been deserted by the enemy for a while. Perhaps our speed had discouraged them, or they had decided the struggle wasn't worth it. Maybe they lost sight of us in the dark. Maybe an angel tripped them or something of greater importance diverted them. I have no doubt that God powered our flight because of Psalm 86:7: "In the day of trouble I will call upon thee: for thou will answer me."

Not only were my friend and I intact, but her dad and brother were police officers! Immediately they listened, snapped into action, and left the house to find the group that had caused our awful ordeal.

My friend and I were left with an abundance of emotion, hearts pumping with adrenaline, chests burning, heaving to breathe, but no greater emotion than our gratitude for the precious love of God!

God kept us from the devil's tactics that night. I am much older now and have experienced the miraculous hand of God many times. He is with us always. He loves all people, and desires that all people come to Him, and live forever with Him.

I hope those young assailants have repented of their sins and are now children of Almighty God.

The days passed quickly following our harrowing escape, and soon Christmas arrived. I was shocked when I opened the gift from Mama. Somehow, even with our destitute means, she managed to get the doll I so adored!

Many miles we traveled to Idaho. Unfortunately, the period we spent there was another chapter with the same theme as our prior experiences. Daddy's ambition did not translate into a financial pot of gold and our affairs only burdened Mama with more worries to endure, and inevitably rivaled the past.

The bluebirds didn't fly over the rainbow for us in Idaho, nor did we find the end of the rainbow, but we had a lot of experiences that, though difficult at the time, became blessings.

I met a lot of pupils and my good teacher and learned a lot about people. And, again, God saved me and my friend in the terrible situation that could have ended unhappily.

Finally, however, Mama and Daddy re-packed the car and turned the car back toward the snow-capped mountains and narrow roads on the long, steep, winding, return trip to Kansas.

The Yellow Brick Road Crumbles

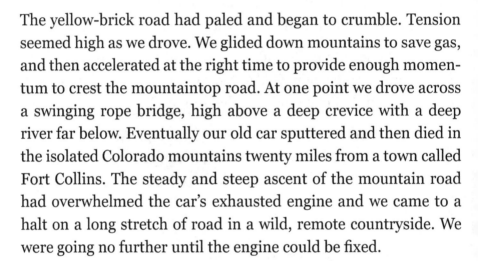

The yellow-brick road had paled and began to crumble. Tension seemed high as we drove. We glided down mountains to save gas, and then accelerated at the right time to provide enough momentum to crest the mountaintop road. At one point we drove across a swinging rope bridge, high above a deep crevice with a deep river far below. Eventually our old car sputtered and then died in the isolated Colorado mountains twenty miles from a town called Fort Collins. The steady and steep ascent of the mountain road had overwhelmed the car's exhausted engine and we came to a halt on a long stretch of road in a wild, remote countryside. We were going no further until the engine could be fixed.

Daddy found a solitary house almost hidden from the road by the profuse foliage and abundance of evergreen and over-grown pine trees embedded in the lonely, extensive cluster of hills that surrounded them. An older couple lived there, and they had an older, husky son with strange traits who walked crooked and bow-legged—just like the sailors we read about who spent years walking on the decks of ships rocked by the sea. They agreed that we could live in a log cabin they owned that was a distance away in the hills if we children would run in their cows each night. They told Daddy the cabin had running water.

We found the cabin, an original frontiersman's, or hunter's cabin. We moved into the old rough-hewn log cabin with the shrunken wood shingles that were curled up at the edges or splintered or both. This was the ninth house I lived in. It did indeed have running water—a shallow creek bed that ran right in front of the house. Most mornings presented a light drizzle of rain, yielding an occasional cup of dirty water. The window openings had no glass, which was frightening with wild animals living so free in the vicinity. Teeny-tiny flying insects that craved blood welcomed us; they would freely investigate the most delicate parts of our bodies and dine wherever they pleased, leaving us with nothing but constant itching. The one good fortune was an ancient cast-iron, wood-burning stove that was functional for cooking.

We hoped it wouldn't take a long time to figure out the problem with the car, and then be able to obtain the parts required to repair it.

The surrounding mountains didn't seem to move, the hills were consistently inconsistent, and deep gullies curved in sneaky seclusion through the landscape. Herding up the cows each evening required much ambitious effort. Every step you took was seemed to slant upwards, pulling on the calf and leg muscles. Covering the area where the cows ranged required every muscle in the body. It was difficult to locate the cows in such a huge area, and then surround them and try to keep them in a group headed to the barn over the hills. It would be hard enough if you rode a horse, but we were on foot! If the son had walked the hills after those cows for so long, it was no wonder that his legs had grown bow-legged to accommodate the constant rises and struggles demanded just to contain the energetic—I'm being nice here—wild animals.

We children ran barefoot across the mountain slopes vigorously to chase in the wild, scattered cattle, exercising caution with the bull. I think those cows enjoyed being chased, they ran excitedly, frivolously as if it was a game to remain independent, tossing their heads and bawling mockingly. We were always concerned the bull would get agitated and provoke an incident; we didn't want to encounter a bristling wall of angry rawhide and powerful, sharp horns. There weren't any large trees in the pastures to climb; the herd had scarfed it all down to what now was mostly scrub, scruffy trees, and tall weeds.

It wasn't a pleasant task and we dreaded it, but we persisted. The constant risk of walking upon slithery, huge, rattle snakes and vicious, silent predators, including mountain lions, compounded our distress.

Compared to those possibilities, the sharp-speared cactus faded in comparison—not only was cactus a constant threat, but it grew like grass and covered the ground with its prickly thorns. Those sharp thorns didn't pull out of the tender skin easily! Not even the leathery soles of our bare feet were immune to their painful intrusions. Pulling and twisting out those thorns was an agonizing effort.

The herd had to be milked at a certain time each day, and we didn't want to see the shadows begin to stretch over the hills, fearing not only loss of the cows, but the enhanced chance of encountering wild predators sniffing us out for dinner. The deer we saw could disappear in an instant merely by dropping swiftly down into the weeds whose colors rivaled the hides of the deer. It was surreal.

During the days, we children went into the hills and cut reeds for arrows and played cowboys and Indians. Further into the mountain, we discovered an amazing river that was so cool and clear the pebbles shone right through the translucent water. It was surrounded by evergreen trees and the whole scene was a splendor of nature.

We decided to cut fishing poles from surrounding canes of thin trees, tied string to the poles and set about to fish the beautiful water. Some fresh fish to eat sounded fantastic. The bait we used was whatever we could find, including digging for worms however we could.

We had fished for years because fish was a wonderful addition to our diet whenever we caught them. We took fishing very seriously for food; it wasn't sport to us. Unfortunately, our persistence at this river did not prove profitable. My siblings finally decided to go back to the log cabin, but I didn't want to leave. I stayed behind hoping that something would take the bait and I'd have a fish to take home for supper.

The air that day was refreshing, the scenery was astounding, and I was soaking in the whole enjoyable atmosphere, my artist's eyes celebrating the structure of every object—water, rocks, tree, fallen trees—it was a lavishing scene. Until the sound. There was no question about the sound; only one animal makes that sound—a mountain lion. And IT WAS LOUD! Loud and NEAR!

The fishing pole we had cut fell from my shaking hands, my feet flew out of my shoes, and my skinny legs were pumping homeward, my feet collecting cactus thorns as I ran—even trying to jump over them as I skimmed the dry soil, thankful the ground on the mountain was slanting downward. Fear accelerated my flight, and I didn't stop until I reached the old cabin.

OLD CABIN

Oh, it was painful pulling out cactus thorns! My feet were tough, but I still suffered as each thorn was extracted from my feet!

COLORADO
Mt. LION!

One day, the woman from the odd owners of the ancient cabin brought Mama a bucket of pig's innards, suggesting she could cook them for us children. Mama considerately accepted the "gift" but after the woman had gone, Mama threw out the bucket of "pork guts" stating that she would never feed such a thing to her children.

While we lived in that old cabin, I suffered one of the worst toothaches a person could experience. The pain was indescribable and at the time, I felt I could not bear it. My cheek swelled into a painful abscess and the pain was debilitating and persistent. There was no relief, and I sank into a hot and damp fever, in a stupor of pain, burning and shaking, with no access to medicine of any kind.

Mama was busy with Stephen because he was having a serious toothache like mine, his cheek swollen, red and purple. He was about eight years old, so Mama cared diligently for him, wrapping him in a blanket, attempting to break his fever, and rocking him.

I was unable to help myself but since I was close to eleven, Mama must have figured that I could take care of myself. I laid on the thin blanket on the floor of the one-room cabin, and the torture from the pain in my head prevented my ability to rise from the thin blanket and get up from the floor.

I craved help and water, but my situation didn't register with anyone around. Who can know the extent of pain except the person experiencing it? I became too weak and incompetent, so I groaned and moaned and rolled from side to side to stem the violence of the pain and try to divert my focus—anything to try to try to survive the horrible battle raging in my head. I was incapacitated by the monster that now swirled around, the pain clawing into my abdomen with green nausea that took control of my limbs.

The insidious severity of the violent intensity of the pain grew unabated through the millennia of the night and defied rationale thought. The lack of moral support added to the psychological duress and was emotionally devastating. I don't think I went unconscious through the long, crucible of night, but the Angel of God helped me. To this day I can't understand why there was no compassion or solace offered to me. I say that with no blame toward anyone; life was hard, and we did not have the availability of doctors like we do today. We were too far from the town with no way to get there, and we couldn't have afforded one anyway.

Storm Clouds

I wish we had found the rainbow's end. The dreams and hopes of our family began to crumble into fool's gold, then rough gravel, and then dirt. When we reached Kansas, we moved into a little house. I didn't like the house, or anything about it. The spark in our family had been extinguished. The tensions between Daddy and Mama were constant. Things were not right.

Mama had left her treasured photos in a large, old, dome topped trunk under Mary's care (yes, that Mary), and of course, when we returned to Kansas, all of Mama's treasured family photos were gone!

My oldest brother, Randall, who had left us in Idaho, had returned to Kansas and was adopted by a couple who hadn't been able to conceive children. Prior to our family leaving for Idaho, this couple had approached my oldest brother and sister about leaving our family and becoming their children through adoption. The couple had a home and financial means and would support them. I suppose in those days the lack of government regulations allowed for such arrangements.

I didn't know any of this at the time. Although Randall and I were many years apart as children, I was always so fond of him.

I just knew my brother I cared for was gone. Mama was so hurt that he was now someone else's "son" that she forbade the rest of us children from speaking his name or making any reference to him. She would tell people that she had eleven children.

My oldest sister told me years later of this situation, and that she was tempted to leave as well given the prospect of a better living situation but could not leave Mama in such a way.

One day Randall drove up in his car, but Mama wouldn't speak to him. I didn't see him again for forty years. His absence left a deep wound in my heart.

My oldest sister got a job, worked hard, and saved some money. She bought an old car, and one day up and left and moved back to Idaho. I missed her but I was hopeful that she would have a wonderful life.

I also heard that the Moore's—the pleasant couple that the horses and turkeys—had fell upon hard times. Mr. Moore's financial venture comprised of his flock of prized turkeys collapsed when the turkeys were smitten with a disease and they all died. The enterprise had been financed with a mortgage on the farm. Unable to pay the mortgage, the Moore's lost their farm and savings and had to move to town. It was quite sad.

At school, I was in the class of one of my brother's prior teachers in grade school, after he had been her student. Their relationship had been one of hostility, and she was so determined to reap vengeance on me, that she emotionally devastated me on several occasions. I was so negatively affected because I was a sensitive child. The emotional pain I was accumulating was unbearable and I began to have thoughts of suicide.

My faithful God helped me as I walked home from class one day, telling me what to do to change the situation. I worked diligently and each day I treated her with purposeful dignity and respect, no matter what she did. Soon, to my amazement, her whole attitude and behavior towards me changed for the better.

Then we moved, again, to a small house in the country. We lived there a fleeting time; one night my sister awoke screaming, swearing that she saw a ghost. We then moved to another house in the country, miles away from the "ghost" house.

This next house was an ancient farmhouse—old, worn, and cold. We drew water from an outside well. We girls slept upstairs and every night the stairs creaked—one after another—as if someone were walking upstairs. That scared us and we would put the quilts up over our heads. But there was never anyone on the stairs.

The crooked windows rattled, and the house had been built and then, appeared to have been built on to. It was a mysterious house. We had a pot-belly stove in the front living room, where we tried to keep warm. Mama hung clothes lines above the stove to dry the laundry. There was no electricity; coal-oil lamps were our light. The old coal-oil lamps helped us see, but the black smoke arising from the flame of the burning wick blackened the glass lamp so quick that a bright light didn't last long.

Our school was at the nearest country school. My two older sisters and I were on the girls' basketball for two years at this school, and our team never lost a game to any competing school teams. Our coach was a decent man and treated us with respect while persistently demanding our seriousness. We were committed and intent, learning the game, handling the ball, and mastering the plays. Our coach also taught us to be principled when playing other teams; we never made underhanded moves or tried to cheat. The school league required all girls playing basketball to cut their fingernails to the fingertips; it was common for some teams to severely scratch their opponents. We never lowered our character to behave in such a manner. We just worked hard, constantly, and that's why we won.

Our coach knew we were poor, although nothing was said about it. One night he came to our house, knocked at the front door, and humbly handed several bags of food to Mama, mumbling something about some farm meeting having too much food. He came and left in a generous flash, as if he did not want to embarrass Mama. He never mentioned it at practice.

We rarely had the books and pencils and papers that we needed for school, and in those days such things were not provided to all students. I also didn't realize I needed glasses; I just knew that I couldn't read most of what written on the chalkboards unless I was quite near the board.

Mama worked hard to keep us clean and neat, but it was so difficult. We had no electricity, no running water, and our toilet was an out-house. Toilet paper was a luxury, so catalogs and newspapers were repurposed, even though stiff and unpleasant.

Mama Grizzly

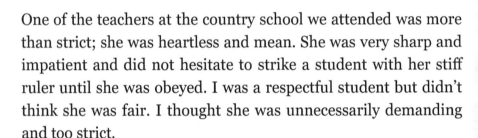

One of the teachers at the country school we attended was more than strict; she was heartless and mean. She was very sharp and impatient and did not hesitate to strike a student with her stiff ruler until she was obeyed. I was a respectful student but didn't think she was fair. I thought she was unnecessarily demanding and too strict.

One day, when this teacher was the attendant at the door into the school building during outdoor recess, I desperately needed to use the girl's bathroom. I wasn't one of the "rich" girls who luxuriated in front of the mirrors, admiring their latest fashionable clothes. This mean teacher would not allow me inside to use the bathroom and nature was not going to wait. I ran to find my sister, Rachel, telling her the situation. Rachel returned with me to the entrance. The teacher extended her arm rigidly so that I could not enter. Undaunted, Rachel glared at the teacher and said resolutely, "move your arm or I will bite it in half." The teacher let her arm down and I quickly proceeded to the bathroom.

One day at school, while I was in the class of a different teacher, I was quietly writing answers for the day's lessons. A soft knock on the door interrupted the industrious quiet of our classroom. With curiosity, our teacher answered the door, then motioned for me to come forward. In the doorway stood Stephen, my little brother. His was particularly upset. Though unsure of the situation, the kind teacher allowed me the respect to speak alone with Stephen, closing the classroom door for the sake of our privacy.

There in the hallway stood Stephen—a thin, hungry, little boy, brown hair askew, wearing old, torn, jeans too big for him, bunched up at the waist by a belt that hung beyond his skinny waist. The stained shirt, much too large, is tucked partially into the jeans. The shirt is crooked—a button is missing, and another button is in the wrong buttonhole because of the button that has been torn off. His dark skin shows through the open holes and walnut stains cover his hands.

His ankles bare of socks, his old, scruffy shoes too large—but they are the nearest size Mama could find for him. The shoes noisily slap the floor when he walks, his feet trying to find some grip on the cardboard inserted to cover the holes in the soles.

My little brother, with such a tender heart, looked up at me with his large, deep brown eyes, brimming with sadness, as he tried to maintain composure.

"My teacher said I stink."

A heartless, mean teacher had humiliated him in front of the class with her harsh comments. He was so upset—lip quivering as tears rimmed his eyelashes. And I was indignant. I excused myself from class, instructed Stephen to wait in the hallway, and I took off running for home. Home was a couple of miles away, but

I arrived there quickly. I told Mama what the teacher had said to Stephen.

Mama grabbed her coat, comprised of old wool fabric, stiff and uncomfortable, having long outlived its prior fashion. Mama took care of her coat, second-hand as it was, but the worn fabric was still prone to tear and wrinkle. Many stitches patched portions of the coat—rips repaired, and missing buttons replaced by Mama's thread and needle—all announcing the presence of poverty.

Mama was a kind and gentle soul who loved God. She would often quote poems and told her children meaningful stories. But mistreat a child of hers? Mother Grizzly was walking back to the school with me.

We arrived at the school, and I pointed out Stephen's classroom. Mama didn't knock; she entered with intent. Her back was straight, her chin held high, shoulders back, and lightning was in her eyes.

Mama never resorted to profanity and did not need to: her verbal ability could skin a wildcat in situations like these. When she was outraged by disrespect or cruelty, her amazing intellect would craft speech that cut through any arguments or attempts to discredit her opinions.

The next few moments became a day remembered by all attending that country school. Mama confronted Stephen's teacher with spectacular strength and incredible oratory. This was a speech of passion, her voice so loud that it reverberated through our country school. Students and teachers came into the hallway to witness what was happening. Then the students began cheering for Mama! Applause filled the hallway. The entire school was so inspired to see someone stand up to this merciless teacher. When Mama was finished, that teacher had no confusion about the consequence of picking on Mama's children—no matter our social status.

Mama walked all those miles - in her old coat.
Then the school rocked!

Later in the school year, my other brother, Daniel, somehow charmed this teacher with his feigned pleasant demeanor when he invited her to ride the merry-go-round in the school yard. She seated herself amongst the students that sat on the fun spinning device and smiled at my brother. Appearing cheerful and polite, my brother slowly began to push the merry-go-round. I was surprised at his behavior, as this was not his usual manner.

Quietly, unnoticeably, in a few minutes, not only was my brother pushing a bit faster, but all the other students had left their places on the merry-go-round, and were spread about the grass, watching the scene.

To my astonishment, my brother began to run faster, pushing the merry-go-round faster and faster and faster! I didn't know what was happening—the teacher was spinning so fast, that she was losing hold on the round, metal, bar that served as a handgrip and the velocity prevented her body any leverage on the wooden seat. Daniel was now running as fast as he could—the merry-go-round was circling at a dizzying pace. The teacher's grip slipped as the centrifugal force increased until, helpless, she flew off the merry-go-round and into the barbed wire fence that separated the school yard from the adjacent cow pasture.

She was so discombobulated, and thankfully only ripped her nylon hose! Shaking, she went into her classroom and put fingernail polish on the hose tears, to prevent any worse damage. I was flabbergasted.

For Daniel, it was payback for how she had humiliated Stephen.

Home Alone

The constant challenge of feeding her children weighed heavily on Mama. In those days, government assistance was not an option if and adult man lived in the home. One day she went to see the pastor of the church she walked us to each Sunday. She sought his advice regarding whether to divorce Daddy so she could receive government assistance. The pastor told her that if she divorced Daddy, she would not be welcome to return to the church.

His words hurt my mother severely. She had tried to be a God-fearing woman, faithfully teaching her children truths from the Bible, and walking us several miles each way to attend church service each Sunday.

She did divorce Daddy. And we didn't return to church.

In later years, Mama would go to church and sit towards the back. She always left early, wanting to avoid any encounter that would make her feel ashamed.

Before the school year was out, we moved again; this was the twelfth house I lived in. Daddy was gone. It would be decades before I saw Daddy again. None of us understood the dynamics of the strange situation. We were told only to never mentioned Daddy again and had no idea where Daddy had gone.

Mama got a telephone, and she and Daddy would argue over the phone, threatening each other. Our old, safe, world was over. A new one was beginning—and it wasn't good.

Mama couldn't afford another bed, so I slept on a very thin cotton "mattress" atop a flat, wired bed frame. I didn't even think about it, after years of sleeping on a blanket laid on the floor.

My older siblings had already left home or were on the verge of leaving to find their own way in life. I wondered how my one older sister had so many clothes in her large closet, when I had so few clothes. She did not share either. Not even a belt. She was harsh and unkind. She was gone most of the time, dating a young man she soon would marry.

My other sister, Rachel, decided to do whatever, whenever she decided. She wasn't concerned about her clothes or much of anything. One night, she borrowed a can-can—a bustling half-slip to make skirts stand out—from my clothes-hoarding sister, Lucy, to go on a date. I doubt that Lucy was aware of the borrowing. While Rachel and her date were driving down the road, she threw the frilly, ruffled can-can out the car window and had no concern of sisterly consequences as the frilly slip flew away in the wind.

Mama was frequently gone to secret places. I believe Mama was doing the best she could. She was determined to owe no one any money. I never blamed Mama, and I have more respect for her than most women in the world, knowing her prior life had been so brutally hard. Still, her frequent absences allowed the devil to joyfully move into our fragile home.

Unknown to us, she was dating a man named Johnny, who already had children of his own. She became involved in a totally different family. We remaining children had no ideas as to why or where she disappeared so much and for so long—sometimes for days. I know she was affected by her conscience, and that it had to be difficult for her to maintain two separate worlds. Eventually we children became aware of Johnny's existence, and supposed Mama was with him when she was gone. Mama never allowed Johnny to move into our house. She lived a portion of her life in his house, mixing with his family and children who we did not know.

I was the oldest child consistently at home, so I was expected to take care of everything. I took on many baby-sitting jobs for which I received no pay—any compensation went directly to Mama. Life at home was bizarre and distressing.

I was nearly thirteen years of age when I learned about menstruation. One day, I felt a torrent of sticky fluid flowing down my legs. I examined the situation, and the flood of blood convinced me I that I was dying. I grabbed the first available cloth nearby and tried to stench the blood. Unfortunately, I had grabbed a slip that belonged to my clothes-hoarding sister. When she and Mama came up the stairs to my emotional screams, my angry sister scorched my hide for using her slip!

Mama gave me some money and sent me to the drugstore to buy items for menstruation, which I knew nothing about. I walked to the drug store, hoping the blood would stop before I arrived. I was terribly embarrassed to ask for the items when I got to the store, but the clerk was kind and helpful, and I learned about the natural process of menstruation.

Mama was now receiving welfare benefit aid, but it was a small amount. These were the days when receiving welfare was the same as the government inscribing a large tattoo on your forehead with a symbol meaning "food stamp tramps." Those on welfare were considered social leaches, inept, valueless, and lazy beggars. The shame associated with receiving welfare was so humiliating that it replaced any sense of self-value in our psyche with the imprint of worthlessness.

The move to this house meant attending a different school. School was terrible. The girls in my grade were becoming interested in boys and clothes. We children still went to school with charity, hand-me-down clothes and very seldom had school supplies. Even though I didn't have most of the materials I needed, I worked as best I could. Many of the teachers and students were nice people; some were not. I learned several lessons in school. One of them most of the pupils didn't believe: our teacher said she got her white hair when she was in a military project where she, as well as others, were sent under water to examine for something, and at the bottom of the dam, she saw a catfish so large that it frightened her so much, her hair turned white over-night.

After school, I returned home to watch over my younger siblings. Our constant state of confusion in an environment now lacking consistent direction, constructive activities, and restraints, opened the door to wild behavior. Initially, their antics were just fun and games. They didn't know what to do with themselves and began to look to me for knowledge or direction that I did not have to give. I was expected to legislate Mama's expectations for the family, but I was given no official authority. I might have been partially effective if Mama had worked with me and helped me understand our new situation. However, she kept us in the dark. I wish I had known what was happening.

Mama's indiscretions and the societal challenges we children experienced produced an environment of disorientation that compromised the foundation of meaning, value, and discipline in my younger siblings. They began to lose themselves in the turmoil. When Mama was present and expected their discipline and obedience, they were grateful, but also uncertain and confused.

Each child handled the situation differently. Some of my siblings remained mellow and accepting, though confused. Others became visibly angry; my one brother became a volcano of extremely intense emotions. The simmering consequences would explode when we were living in the next house.

The Junk Yard House

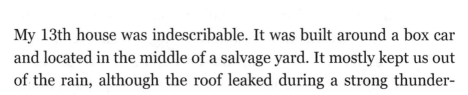

My 13th house was indescribable. It was built around a box car and located in the middle of a salvage yard. It mostly kept us out of the rain, although the roof leaked during a strong thunderstorm. The only water we had was when Johnny hauled some to the parking area and filled a large, round, plastic barrel. We drew our water from that barrel for all our needs.

We lived in this salvage-yard boxcar house owned by Johnny—a man we still had not met. Adjacent to the dwelling was a small patch of gravel and dirt that served as a yard. We were instructed that the house and yard were the only areas we were allowed to inhabit.

Life went on all around us, as Johnny sold car parts, but we weren't a part of his world and had no knowledge of it. He had a building at the other end of the road mid-way through the salvage yard where he conducted his business.

There was no bathroom inside the house. To get ready for school, I fetched two buckets of water from the plastic barrel and carried them back to the house. I attempted to heat water from one bucket on the undependable gas stove in a small area that served as a kitchen. I then proceeded outside, carrying the two buckets of warm and cold water to an old shack of a building that had no doors and faced the highway. Here I would try to take a shower. I would scrunch myself as small as I could, hoping the traffic on the highway would not give anyone a view of me. At least, the cars and trucks speeding by weren't that close to the shack.

After washing with the warm water and soap, I would douse myself with the second bucket of ice-cold water. After drying off, I would get dressed for school. Even when it was freezing outside, this was my routine. I then rounded up my younger siblings, and we trekked up the road to catch the school bus, usually without the needed school supplies or money for lunches.

And so I began the ninth grade. The first day of school, while we were seated at our alphabetical desk in science class, a handsome young man turned towards me and winked at me. I ignored him, not wanting to be seen as flirtatious.

His name was Trent. He was different than the other young men in school. He was always decent and respectful of me, and a warmth began to grow in my heart for him. We developed a bond that was unusual for people our age.

He was on the football and basketball teams at school and was one of the best players. He was very intense and competitive, and always played with good sportsmanship. I tried to attend as many of his sports games as I could, given my home situation.

When it was lunchtime at school, I usually had no lunches. I didn't know I could have asked for government relief lunches. That would have been shameful to me, anyway.

Occasionally, when Mama gave me some money, a friend and I would go and eat uptown at the restaurant—I usually ordered an inexpensive salad. Then, there was a nice girl who befriended me and took me to her home to eat lunch, until her mother put a stop to that. With little or no food for my school lunch, I would wander from place to place throughout the building, scavenging any leftover food I might find while hoping to capture no one's gaze. Lunch hour was agonizing.

Shoes were hard to come by, as well. We children wore whatever shoes we could get, regardless of fit. Many times, we would put cardboard in our soles to accommodate the holes in the shoes. At school I was careful to keep my feet flat on the floor so no one would see the holes in the bottom the soles.

Living on the salvage yard, our sense of being outcasts was amplified by how Mama's boyfriend, Johnny, treated us. We barely had any interaction with him, but it was obvious we were not accepted by him; we just lived in the shadows. Years later I discovered that he had two children, whom he provided for extravagantly during the same years we lived in the box car house.

Our family's isolation and life as outcasts in society affected each of us children differently. A couple of my brothers became indifferent—"If I can't be a part of society, I'll do whatever I want." They began to sneak alcohol into the house and doing drugs. This was exacerbated by us now being fatherless. We were told Daddy was not allowed to be near us "for assistance' sake."

Bickering and fighting and violence became a frequent occurrence between my siblings. As I was the oldest of us who were present in the house each day, I attempted to fill the parental void, to ill effect. My reprimands and encouragements were met with violations and defiance; I was so young that my authority was laughable. I felt ineffective, although I know I was able to guide and protect them to a small extent. In tandem with this, I was attempting to do well in school and was working small jobs on the side for money that I would give to Mama. I was so confused about the turn of events in life; I was in constant quandary.

My brother, Daniel, who was a year or so younger than me, was so, so angry. The anger and emptiness that had simmered for so long began to explode. He and our younger brother, Stephen, fought each other all the time. Our lives had become intolerable.

One day I came upon them fighting, but never to this degree. Daniel was enraged, and his blows were more than forceful. Stephen was trying to fend them off, but to no avail.

Daniel was beyond control, and I thought he was going to kill our skinny, little brother.

I was unable to talk any sense into Daniel, so I jumped between them and told him to take out his wrath on me. He paused—his eyes full of confusion. I kept telling him to "hit me, hit me." Eventually, he seemed to come to his senses and backed off.

Years later, after high school, Stephen joined the military. After his service, he worked hard to provide for two daughters that he adored. He struggled with alcohol, and decades later asked me once, while he was drunk, why hadn't I protected him from Daniel those many years ago.

He forgot that I did.

However, I could not be home all the time to watch over my younger siblings. In the summers, I worked many hours to benefit Mama's small fund.

The summer after ninth grade, I was hired out to babysit the three small children of a family in town at their house. Sometimes Trent would come to the house, and we would take the children for outdoor activities. The mother of the children gave Mama a glowing report on my "wonderful boyfriend." To my dismay, the woman paid me with fabric at the end of the summer. I don't know if she paid Mama with money.

At home we had an old sewing machine—the type you operated without electricity. I made a dress from one of the pieces of fabric, constructing it without a pattern since I had no money to purchase one. When I wore the dress to school, my home economics teacher asked me what pattern I had used for my dress. I told her I had made the dress without a pattern. She became truly angry with me, thinking I was lying to her. She was hostile towards me for the remainder of the semester.

Throughout all my school years, my siblings and I experienced a common theme: because of our apparent poverty many teachers assumed we lacked intellect and industriousness, or even worse, that we were deviant.

Tenth grade was the same dynamic as the prior year. I worked hard on my studies, though lacking books and simple things like paper and pencils.

One hot fall day, in English class, I was sitting behind Trent. I suppose I was bored or feeling a bit spirited, as I took my pen with red ink and quickly placed a dot on the back of Trent's neck.

He lightly slapped the back of his neck, thinking it was an insect—which was common as we had open windows as the classrooms had no air conditioning. So, I proceeded with another red dot, and another, as it was obvious that Trent thought he was dealing with the antics of a flying insect. In the following class period, his math teacher, seeing the "rash" on the back of his neck, asked Trent if he was feeling sick.

In the middle of winter, one day Trent asked me to join him to walk to the nearby downtown during lunch period. I was hesitant, telling him I was concerned about falling on the ice. He promised to catch me if I slipped, so I went with him. Sure enough, I slipped on the ice—not purposefully! And Trent did not catch me. Awkwardly, he helped me get back on my feet. Later he would tell me he wasn't sure where he should grab me.

The summer after tenth grade, I car-hopped at a drive-in restaurant in town, serving fast food to people in their cars. After work, I begged the other workers for rides home. Sometimes my older brother, Kevin—he was rarely at home, and I had no idea where he spent his time—would pick me up. The other young men at the restaurant tried to shame him by making fun of his car. Kevin had built his own car out of salvaged parts. His car didn't look as nice as the cars other kids had. They didn't recognize the amazing accomplishment of building a working vehicle by piecing together the salvage from a bunch of different cars; something that none of the other young men could have likely achieved.

Eleventh grade arrived. The only good part of my life was Trent.

Trent and I were both taught that affection was inappropriate, so we did not have a good understanding of healthy and suitable affection. One summer night, Trent and I went to the drive-in movies with one of his friends and his friend's date. During the movie, the couple was affectionately enjoying each other's company—what we called "smooching" in those days. Trent and I just quietly watched the movie. Eventually, Trent's friend turned to him and said "Trent, if you don't kiss Jasmine, I will." Trent turned to me and kissed me. Sort-of. As I said, neither of us grew up where affection was displayed.

Living in the boxcar house on the salvage yard was embarrassing, but Trent never had any disdain for my home circumstance. Sometimes he would come pick me up, and we would take my brothers to go play football or do something fun. Trent always treated my family members with respect, never looking down on them. My younger brother, Stephen, came to consider Trent a closer brother than any of his brothers by blood. Later in life, Stephen—a seasoned veteran—hugged Trent tightly and tried to find words to tell Trent how much he loved him. Stephen struggled with alcohol, as did my sister Rachel. They both had such tender hearts. Alcohol was their way to numb the emotional pain, still embedded within from childhood. A short while after that meaningful hug, Stephen would die a premature death.

The third summer a local dentist hired me to be his assistant. I mixed the mercury and some other chemical for people's fillings—silver, I think. My paycheck went to the family. I never resented Mama for using the money I made at these jobs.

I lived in the boxcar house for three years—my ninth, tenth, and eleventh grade years in school. Then, just before my senior year, we moved once again.

The Ring

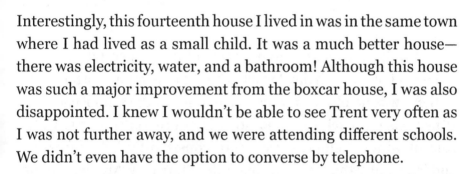

Interestingly, this fourteenth house I lived in was in the same town where I had lived as a small child. It was a much better house—there was electricity, water, and a bathroom! Although this house was such a major improvement from the boxcar house, I was also disappointed. I knew I wouldn't be able to see Trent very often as I was not further away, and we were attending different schools. We didn't even have the option to converse by telephone.

One day a piano showed up in our house. Mama had gotten an old upright piano from someone. In my spare time—which was infrequent—I taught myself how to play the piano by ear from listening to an old 45rpm record—a German polka—in the key of D flat.

I began my senior year in a much larger high school. I don't know how I did it, but I managed to buy school supplies for the twelfth grade, and actually had some books. Again, there were some good teachers and some not-so-good teachers.

Somehow, within the ranks of the seniors, I was considered a "smart" student. Of course, there were many of the typical high school groups, including the "popular girls." Belonging to their group meant that you would benefit by being entitled to their popular influence and importance.

As the "privileged elite," this small, entrenched group initiated and controlled a lot of the activities in the school. The involvement of other students was limited to the approval or disapproval of this popular coterie if it intersected with their world.

The popular girls approached me to inform me I could be "popular" if I allowed them to copy my test papers. I had not interested in being "popular" or to belong to their clique. We did not share the same values and principles.

I walked a distance to high school four times a day, several miles each way. Each day I walked back home for a meager lunch, as there was no money for me to eat lunch at the school cafeteria. I then walked back to school for the afternoon sessions. In the cold of winter, temperatures were consistently below freezing, and frequently they were in single-digit territory. My class immediately after lunch was typing, but on these freezing winter days, my fingers were too stiff to type for the first twenty minutes or so. I received poor grades in that class as a result—but guess who's typing this manuscript!

Two of my teachers sincerely believed in my ability and encouraged me to expand into a career. With their involvement, I had a job lined up as a job as a secretary to a lawyer prior to graduation.

At home, I was busy with watching over the younger siblings, doing homework, cooking, laundry, and other chores. Trent would drive more than thirty minutes to see me whenever he could; most of the time we spent together was on weekends.

He was in his senior year at the other school and worked hard and continuously at his home. His family milked many cows for a living—an enterprise that left little spare time.

After experiencing so many people who were lazy or mean or untrustworthy, I was determined that if I married, it would be to a good, decent, and moral man, who would take care of his family. I found those qualities in Trent, and we slowly learned about each other through the school years that we had spent together. The year we were separated by distance and time did not change our feelings for each other.

When I was walking home for lunch one cold day, one of the students who was on the economical end of the "popular" group spectrum, was picked up by her mom and they offered me a ride home.

Mistakenly, I accepted, surprised that this girl that I knew from school would offer me a ride. When we arrived at my house, they were obviously startled to see the house. Our houses were always in disarray, and on the poorer scale.

Mama couldn't afford to repair screens that were torn, or doors that were crooked, or even paint. One day I had studied the hamburger Mama was frying in the skillet. Mama had to buy the cheap brand because she couldn't pay a few more dollars for a more selective, higher quality choice. As the skillet heated, it began to sizzle as the patties shrank into grease. But what choice did we have when every penny was precious.

After seeing my home, the girl never bothered to acknowledge me again. As if this arrogant attitude from the young high school group wasn't bad enough, some of the teaching staff favored this behavior and allowed it. However, none of this mattered to me. I just did my schoolwork and dreamed about the wonderful guy that I loved.

Graduation night came and all the class was celebrating with a gathering at school. I was beyond happy—I was thrilled! Not because of graduation, but because the kind, smart, handsome young man that I loved had asked me to marry him and gave me a sparkling, beautiful diamond ring to wear on my left hand. We were engaged! That meant everything to me. Many of my fellow students were congratulating us.

It was important to me and Trent to retain our honor amidst our normal passions, and we wanted to save our physical union for our marriage. It was also important to us that we have a church wedding and state our vows before God. We met with the pastor of the church Trent's family attended and decided to get married within the month.

It was important to me to be married before God in the church. Trent and I met with the pastor at Trent's church about getting married.

Our wedding was not of the picture from a fairy book kind. Our families were not enthusiastic about our marriage. All the money I earned went to Mama, so Trent practically paid for everything, selling some of the cows he raised to help pay for the wedding.

Neither of our families wanted us to get married. Mama would be losing me as the principal person taking care of my younger siblings, as well as the income from the jobs I was working. When she realized the wedding was going to happen, she wanted me and Trent to just go to a justice of the peace and get our marriage certificate. She didn't want us to have a church wedding, partly because she didn't have any money to contribute—although we didn't expect that of her. Trent's family wasn't too thrilled about us getting married either and didn't contribute any effort. Trent's sister loaned me her wedding dress, which required several repairs. I made the repairs, which was time-consuming and costly. I don't know why I didn't think about making my own wedding dress—although it would have been difficult to obtain the fabric.

Fortunately, my wonderful friend's mother helped me plan the wedding and organized a lovely reception for us. Regardless of our families' not supporting us, Trent and I were thrilled on the day of our wedding. I was so nervous, I fixed my gaze upon the handsome, loving face of the man I loved. Jubilance flooded my heart as we shared our vows, filtering out the attitudes of those who were negative about our being married.

Over sixty years later, I have never lost the thrill I experienced on that day when we began our life together.

The Divine Encounter

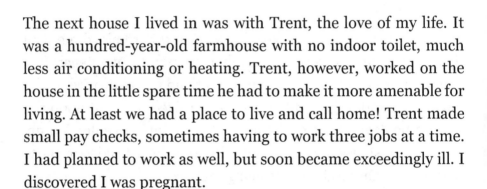

The next house I lived in was with Trent, the love of my life. It was a hundred-year-old farmhouse with no indoor toilet, much less air conditioning or heating. Trent, however, worked on the house in the little spare time he had to make it more amenable for living. At least we had a place to live and call home! Trent made small pay checks, sometimes having to work three jobs at a time. I had planned to work as well, but soon became exceedingly ill. I discovered I was pregnant.

Almost a year after our marriage we had our first child, a baby boy, and just shy of two years later, we had a beautiful baby girl. I loved my children dearly and had hoped for more children; however, I had severe, life-threatening complications during pregnancy and birth. Between the births of my son and daughter, I experienced the tragedy of giving birth to a stillborn child at full term. The doctor advised me to never become pregnant again.

The first five years of our marriage I battled with debilitating illness while trying to be the mother I hoped to be to my young children. It was hellish, and I had only Trent to help me and the children while he was also working so hard to support our new family.

One day I was in the kitchen preparing lunch when I emotionally fell apart. Trent was at work and my children were playing in the living room. In desperation, I cried out to God amid deep depression and hopelessness.

The day was gray, and the sunshine could not penetrate the clouds, covering the sky like a coat of gray paint. I said, "God, if you are real as I've always believed, please help me." I could not stop crying; a dam had burst inside me, and the flood of tears threatened to drown me.

Suddenly, a small ray of light pierced the gray, stolid sky. It streamed into the kitchen through the old, crooked window. For a moment, I couldn't believe what I saw just happened. I dismissed that it had been a message for me. Who was I?

I was awed, but then disbelief set in. I began to peel potatoes when I felt the push of a hand on my shoulder from behind me. Somehow, I knew it was an angel. Then I heard these words: "Go and read your Bible."

"No," I responded. "I don't understand it."

"GO AND READ YOUR BIBLE," the angel commanded, again pushing my shoulder.

This time I set aside my reluctance and walked over to the side table, where I kept the large white Bible that Mama gave us for our wedding.

I kneeled at the side of the table. Not knowing where to read, I simply opened the Bible and pointed at a verse.

Oh, thou of little faith, wherefore did thou doubt?

The scripture penetrated my heart. The words were not condemning, they were liberating. I had not doubted his promises, but I had doubted that they were available to me. All my life I had doubted I was good enough for God, even though I believed in Him. I thought I was too poor, too insignificant, too little to be able to truly please God. I thought people who led certain lives, had money, and consistently follow the regulations of the church were the only ones who truly pleased God.

But in that moment, I realized that God loved me. He wanted me to know this truth. That Jesus' sacrifice was for me. That Jesus loved me.

For the first time in my life, I understood. I prayed, sobbing, that Christ would forgive my sins and enter my heart. And he did. When I arose from kneeling, and praying, my life was changed. I encountered a hope that I had never known.

Then God, in His magnificence, revealed His Word of salvation to my husband. One day, while he was hunting outdoors, Trent sat down to rest on a tree stump. In that quiet moment, while sitting there, the Word of God spoke to his heart. A verse from the book of Matthew in the Bible came to his mind: "And Jesus called a little child unto him, and set him in the midst of them, and said, 'Verily I say unto you, except ye be converted, and become as little children, ye shall not enter into the kingdom of heaven.'"

Trent had always believed in the doctrine of "being good." If you are good enough, then you can go to heaven. But the Holy Spirit revealed God's truth to him, that salvation was not a matter behaving a specific way—not a matter of not believing in "good"—but rather it was through believing in "God." Trent realized the freeing truth that salvation was not achieved by his deeds but made possible by God's design. The words of Jesus penetrated his heart and soul—when he came home, I knew he had been with God. His face was bright with a new light and a smile of joy. A new hope.

It is an eternal hope.

An Eternal Hope

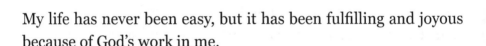

My life has never been easy, but it has been fulfilling and joyous because of God's work in me.

We love Christmas in America. It's so inspiring to see people smiling and singing Christmas carols, and so joyful to see the brightly lit, shiny lights and remember the wonder of God, His love and Grace. Not only feasting on elaborately prepared meals, family sharing and caring, gifting, and lighting candles in church to thank God for all his magnificent creation and love for His creation.

And most of all to celebrate His eternal gift of life. It is more than amazing that the Creator of the entire universe would ponder and determine to create humans—even to create us in His own powerful likeness. And even more, to confer on humans the inscrutable blend of body, spirit and soul.

When Trent and I were drawn to each other, he could not force me to love him, nor could I force him to love me. How unfulfilling it would be if we were just calibrated puppets who only interacted because of a pre-set ordinance of routine, with no capacity for choosing love. How empty and shallow it would be to live life with another in a relationship that is forced upon you.

The risk of choice in companionship also offers the opportunity for fulfillment.

God knew the risk of choice was that his beloved creation—humans—might hate him, deny him, or disobey him, But He desired a relationship with humans that was consensual in love and companionship. He desired for another being to experience the power of love. This was an incredulous phenomenon—an experiment of unbelievable repercussions and proportion. So, God created Adam and Eve. They were provided the abundance and beauty of the world God created and given a single warning by God: the negative consequences that would transpire from the act of eating the fruit of ony one tree.

Then evil marred the brilliance of God's design. Satan—the enemy of God—had a singular goal: to destroy any good thing that God created. Knowing that God treasured human beings more than all, Satan's quest became the destruction and death of each human's eternal soul. He approached Adam and Eve, suggesting to them that God wanted to restrict them from being all they were created to be. Adam and Eve chose to ignore God's warning.

Sin is choosing to act in ways that violate God's laws. These laws are not designed to limit or enslave people, but rather to provide abundance and fulfillment. When Adam and Eve chose to violate God's law, sin was ushered into our world. It was fused into our DNA. The result is a barrier that separates people from God, for one can truly only know God and experience His eternal blessing when nothing separates them from God.

Being separated from God eventually leads to destruction.

Sin is not a matter of choosing "bad" rather than "good." There are many benefits to being "good," but good behavior does not remove the barrier between humans and God. The religions created by mankind throughout history are based on defining "what is good" and "what is bad." They seek to manipulate people rather than set them truly free. Even if one does not adhere to a religion, the belief of "good" as the doorway to heaven is false. "Good" and "bad" are not the basis of the problem, and thus not the solution.

Fortunately, God is merciful, and his love is relentless. God's grace is both powerful and eternal and cannot be limited by the mission of Satan. God provided a way to remove the barrier of sin through His son, Jesus Christ. The only salvation available to reunite humans with God, now and for eternity, is by recognizing the sacrifice Jesus made in His death on the cross, asking for God's forgiveness and accepting Jesus as one's Savior. This simple, yet amazing and life-changing opportunity, eradicates the barrier of sin and opens the door for every person to experience the real and lasting fulfillment in life that God intends for all people. The rich, the poor, the clean, the dirty, the king, the pauper, the hobo, the president—God's offer of salvation is to everyone. Every person is of equal value to God.

A choice—God gives each of us a choice. A choice for eternal life with Him, in heaven where the presence of love and peace and hope and wonder and fulfillment is forever and where sin cannot exist. There is no more crucial decision to make, than to ask forgiveness of your sins and accept Jesus Chris into your heart, while you have the opportunity!

No matter where you are in life, you can pray this prayer, or a prayer in your own words, to open the door to the eternal hope that God has made available to everyone.

Dear God, I open my heart to you. I ask you to forgive me for my sins and to be my Savior forever. I choose to follow Jesus and to live according to Your Word. Help me to know Your hope and to receive Your love.

Epilogue

Life, itself, is indeed a collage of incidents, some good—some extremely tragic. From house to house, through the days of my childhood, the Lord Jesus was always with me. As a young adult, God gave to me a wonderful husband who I have loved all these years. And God, in His mercy, redeemed us both. Our hope and prayer are for you to experience the love of Jesus and witness His miracles throughout your life.

Dillie Road Books

www.dillieroadbooks.com

CPSIA information can be obtained
at www.ICGtesting.com
Printed in the USA
BVHW041352071021
618420BV00013B/646

Journey of Hope is the story of a young girl,
growing up in a family of twelve children, trapped in
extreme poverty and facing repeated social challenges.
Her father and mother search for a better life—
a long, tedious journey that lasts for many years
and spans many miles and many houses, but
hardship continues to multiply.

Against a backdrop of societal rejection, dysfunction and
disillusionment, this young girl clings to hope, leading to
an encounter that changes her life forever.

Dillie Road Books

Jasmine Carol is an author
and prolific artist. To
contact Jasmine, visit
www.dillieroadbooks.com

ISBN 978-1-7379040-0-7

90000

9 781737 904007